The Lincoln-Douglas Debates

James Buchanan, president of the United States at the time of the Lincoln-Douglas debates of 1858. *Courtesy Brady Collection, National Archives.*

The
Lincoln - Douglas
Debates

Frank L. Dennis

Mason & Lipscomb PUBLISHERS   NEW YORK

First Printing

Printed in the United States of America

To Kittie

Library of Congress Cataloging in Publication Data

Dennis, Frank L   1907-
    The Lincoln-Douglas debates.

    (Great events in world history)
    SUMMARY: Analyzes the background of the debates
between two senatorial candidates from Illinois in 1858
and the effect they had on United States history.
    Bibliography: p.
    1. Lincoln-Douglas debates, 1858. 2. Lincoln,
Abraham, Pres. U. S., 1809-1865. 3. Douglas, Stephen
Arnold, 1813-1861. [1. Lincoln-Douglas debates, 1858.
2. Lincoln, Abraham, Pres. U..S., 1809-1865.
3. Douglas, Stephen Arnold, 1813-1861] I. Title.

E457.4.D36   973.6'8   74-4478
ISBN 0-88405-062-9

Contents

List of Illustrations

Foreword

BY CARL ALBERT
Speaker of the U.S. House
of Representatives

I AM PRIVILEGED to have this opportunity to write a foreword to this account of the great Lincoln-Douglas debates written by Frank Dennis, my friend from our days at the University of Oklahoma. Mr. Dennis has given contemporary meaning to this century-old, but always fascinating drama, which proved to be pivotal in American political history. He has described a series of confrontations between two great public speakers, one a distinguished United States senator and national spokesman of the established Democratic party, and the other, the rising star of the young Republican party in the state of Illinois, a free-soil state and testing ground of differing views on the extension of slavery. The similarities between Lincoln and Douglas were greater than their differences; yet when displayed before the voters, their variances were significant enough to divide the nation. The debates propelled Lincoln into national prominence and triggered a chain of events that two years later would make him the Republican candidate for president and eventually the president of a riven and embittered country. Douglas, on the other hand, was to be deprived of the presidency, which he had long sought.

Why were these arguments, conducted in the mud-paved streets of small towns before audiences of frontiersmen sitting in covered wagons or camped in the open air, forums of national importance? One might compare their impact to that of today's nationally televised political debates, which often furnish a showcase from which the audience makes its determinations. There were on the scene at the time several new mediums of information—shorthand reporters, the telegraph, and coverage by big city newspapers. For the first time, millions would read in print what a few thousand had heard the day before.

What they read, of course, was that Lincoln had forced Douglas to reiterate his stand on slavery, thus causing him to lose the support of many strong proslavery advocates from the South. Douglas publicly stated that new territories should decide for themselves whether or not to permit slavery in their areas, rather than insist that slave owners should be able to take their slaves with them wherever they settled. Douglas's articulation of his views on this subject ultimately cost him the presidency. Ironically, Lincoln lost the senatorial race that he had contested with his opponent, but two years later was elected president. The debates not only demonstrated Lincoln's skill as a debater, but his prescience in recognizing in its infancy the issue that was to bring the greatest civil cleavage this country has ever known. The history of the careers of Douglas and Lincoln is absorbing, as is the portrayal of the series of political compromises by which the new nation attempted to deal with the question of slavery in its newly opened lands.

Equally of interest to me is the evidence that historically the essence of our democracy has been participation by the citizens in the democratic process. More than a hundred years ago, tens of thousands of Americans cared enough about important national issues to travel days by boat or horseback or buggy to hear "politicians" debate the pros and cons of such issues. They suffered the discomforts of sitting outdoors in drizzling rain; they endured the hardships of camp life; they roasted oxen in open pits for food—all because they wished to be informed before they voted. Obviously, they placed great value on their right to vote. Would our citizens today make such sacrifices in order to exercise their suffrage? It is hard to know in this era of instant mass communications—newspapers, radio, television—because the question does not arise in the same way.

Surely, this look backward should remind us that our forefathers set great store by their right to participate in the political process and went to considerable lengths to make certain that they participated intelligently. My hope is that today all citizens will regain, if they have not retained, their personal involvement and faith in the democratic process of this republic, in order that they may claim their heritage—the right to listen to and comment on great debates on great issues before our country.

C. A.

The Lincoln-Douglas Debates

1. The Confrontation at Freeport

THEY CAME FROM all around to see and to hear and to be a part of the spectacle scheduled for Friday, August 27, 1858, in Freeport, Illinois, a hundred miles northwest of Chicago, near the Wisconsin and Iowa borders. They came on foot, on horseback, by buggy, by farm wagon, and by special train. Whole families came, bringing their bedding and camping equipment and home-cooked food. They also brought a great curiosity about what the speakers of the day, Abraham Lincoln and Senator Stephen A. Douglas, would say.

These expectant travelers were the plain people of Illinois. Most of them were hardworking farm folk, originally from the northern and northeastern United States, and included a generous sprinkling of recent German and Irish immigrants. There were few or no Negroes, for although Illinois was a free-soil state its laws forbade Negro residence.

When the streams of out-of-towners and townspeople converged near Goddard's Grove, on the edge of town,

3

Stephen A. Douglas, the senator from Illinois, at about the time of the Lincoln-Douglas debates during the election campaign of 1858. Reproduced from the collections of the Library of Congress.

Abraham Lincoln about the time of the Lincoln-Douglas debates of 1858. *Courtesy the Library of Congress.*

the crowd numbered at least 13,000. Some estimated it at 15,000. The population of Freeport, the seat of Stephenson County, normally numbered about 5,000. Most of the people there that day were used to the outdoors; so the mild drizzle and the chill unusual for August were not enough to keep many away.

The immediate reason for the influx into Freeport was the desire of the people to hear what Lincoln and Senator Douglas would say that day in their debate—the second of seven. They wanted to listen to what might be said that would influence their votes in the state election to be held November 2, 1858. On that date the voters would elect state legislators who, in January, 1859, would choose between Lincoln and Douglas for the United States Senate. Either Douglas would continue for six more years, or Lincoln would replace him.

But more than curiosity about politics impelled the farm and village folk to trek to Freeport for the debate. Their most compelling interest was to witness what was certain to be a memorable event and in a sense to be a part of that event. They would be witnesses to a bloodless duel between the two most able stump speakers* of their day. Such public speaking provided entertainment as well as enlightenment for people cut off from easy access to recreation and information. Outside the cities, newspapers were distributed by mail—a slow process. Citizens with a desire to be up-to-date on important subjects looked to "speechifying" for guidance and perhaps for decisive influence, especially in politics. A face-to-face debate between candidates, or "a forensic

---

* The term *stump speaker* was derived from the practice orators had of mounting tree stumps so as to be seen and heard by rural audiences.

duel," as the newspaper cliché had it, was a kind of show like a state fair or a horse race. Being both entertaining and instructive, it was an important event in any community.

The Lincoln-Douglas debates of the late summer and early autumn of 1858 were the most notable example of this uniquely American spectacle. The speakers were the champions of their respective parties in Illinois. Douglas was famous, the national spokesman of the established Democratic party. Lincoln was well known only in Illinois—the up-and-coming challenger and the state's leader of the strong new Republican party. Both men were acknowledged masters of stump speaking. They could make themselves heard to the edges of large crowds in any kind of weather.

What gave the occasion a special magnetism was the importance of the subject. "The great and durable question of the age" (Lincoln's words) was to be discussed. Slavery In 1858 Illinois was the political testing ground of differing views on the extension of slavery. Thus national attention was focused on this senatorial contest.

The opposing candidates were longtime rivals, each having a large following of loyal admirers. Douglas was the invincible Little Giant to scores of thousands of Democrats, who backed him despite the furious opposition of the party's chieftain, President James Buchanan. Lincoln was Honest Abe, supported by large numbers of former Whigs turned Republican. Each man was his party's choice for the U.S. Senate. Douglas hoped to hold onto the office, which had helped to make him the nation's most prominent and controversial politician, and from which he might move to the presidency. Lincoln's modest goal was to move from the local limelight to the national stage and its attendant opportunities for whatever the future might bring.

What Lincoln and Douglas said that day and how the voters reacted could affect the status of slavery everywhere. The question most precisely at issue was what was to be the future of slavery in the western territories then being opened to settlement. The differences between Lincoln and Douglas over what to do about slavery mirrored bitter differences within the country—differences, which, as they intensified, would threaten the Union itself.

Out of 250 years of Negro bondage in America had come violent diversity of belief among the white people about that bondage. In the agricultural South the slave owners principally were the ruling class. Their prosperity was based on slave labor. Federal law protected the ownership of some four million blacks in the 15 states in which slavery had not been outlawed by state action at the time of the Lincoln-Douglas campaign. The slave owners believed that the federal law, as written in the national Constitution and as then interpreted, permitted slave ownership in the territories also.

The whites who opposed slavery were of two principal classes. The *abolitionists* advocated immediate emancipation. They believed slavery to be morally wrong, an evil that should be expunged by any means, including violence. The *moderates* agreed that slavery was a moral wrong, but they recognized that it was legal constitutionally. They had no program for ending slavery *except to confine it to where it then existed* and to hope that time and the course of events would extinguish it.

Abraham Lincoln was the Illinois leader of the

moderates, who constituted the great majority of the young Republican party.

Stephen A. Douglas believed that the people of a territory had a legal right to determine at the territorial stage whether they wanted slavery—then and also when the territory would become a state. This he termed "popular sovereignty." The Democratic party was split over the popular sovereignty doctrine. The Southern Democratic slavocracy was unwilling to concede that the people of a territory could keep slavery out of it.

Thus, these two able men, whose careers had run parallel and then had diverged over the years, now faced each other for the most important debate of their lives.

2. Twenty Years of Rivalry

It was not a fluke of fate that Abraham Lincoln and Stephen A. Douglas were the principals in the historic confrontation of 1858. They had been rivals in Illinois politics for almost a quarter of a century. Lincoln had won their first political skirmish in 1836. As a second-termer in the state legislature from Sangamon County that year, he had managed successfully the Sangamon delegation's campaign to move the state capital from Vandalia to Springfield in Sangamon. Douglas, a first-termer, had maneuvered unsuccessfully to have his town, Jacksonville, the Morgan County seat, made the capital.

Although Lincoln had been the winner in 1836 in competition with Douglas, by 1858 the latter had outdistanced him. Douglas had been a U.S. senator for 11 years and now was a strong contender for the presidency. In contrast, Lincoln had plodded along unspectacularly. The high point of his political career had been a single undistinguished term in the U.S. House of Representatives.

The difference between these two men in party affiliation had helped from the beginning to make them natural rivals at the state level. Lincoln had been a Whig since his initial campaign in 1832. Now he was a leader of the new Republican party, which had superseded the defunct Whig organization. Douglas had been a lifelong Democrat.

There was a curious twist in their respective roles in their great debates of 1858. Lincoln, who campaigned against the extension of slavery, had been born and reared in states where slavery was lawful and generally believed to be compatible with Christian principles. Douglas, who argued for slavery extension if the local voters wanted it, was a native of Vermont. He had grown to manhood in a New England-New York society that opposed slavery as unchristian.

Lincoln had been born into a family of poor Kentucky whites on February 12, 1809. His father, Thomas Lincoln, was an easygoing farmer, who was handy with carpenter's tools. Tom Lincoln was a drifter, partly because white wage earners of his kind could not compete for jobs with the slave labor of the Kentucky, Tennessee, and Indiana frontiers. Such families as the Lincolns, desperately poor, were looked upon with disdain by the blacks. Trusted slaves took care of the homes and fields of their masters. Slaves looked upon such families as the Lincolns, grubbing out an uncertain living, as "poor whites," or even "poor white trash," as their owners might say.

A logical result of such conditions was that people like the Lincolns hated slavery as a matter of self-interest. Slavery denied poor white people the opportunity for more work at better wages. Where there were slaves to do the work, there could be no jobs at good wages for free whites. In common with people everywhere who directly suffer from such a situation, the poor whites of the slave states disliked the visible cause of their disadvantage—in this case, the Negroes. If the Negroes were not there, there would be no Negro slaves. If there were no slaves, there would be better opportunities for the working-class whites. Therefore, the poverty of the whites was attributable to the Negroes. So ran the reasoning.

Abraham Lincoln was aware as a boy of the adverse effect of slave labor on his family's welfare. He later wrote that in 1816, when he was seven years old, his family moved from Knob Creek in Kentucky to Spencer County in Indiana "partly on account of slavery." Such migration was commonplace in that period for people like the Lincoln clan. They had been on the move since the period prior to the American Revolution.

After leaving Kentucky, Thomas Lincoln; his wife, Nancy; and the children, Sarah and Abe, settled in a forest in Indiana. Near Gentryville on Little Pigeon Creek they built a three-sided shed out of poles, logs, and brush. There they subsisted for a year, living on game, while Tom Lincoln cleared a few acres for corn and completed a one-room cabin of logs. Abe, only eight years old, quickly learned to use the ax and began to develop the strength and skill with that tool that later helped to create his "rail-splitter" image.

In a few months relatives of the Lincolns, Tom and Betsy Sparrow, joined them on Little Pigeon Creek. The Sparrows lived in the open-face shelter, the Lincolns in the cabin. They farmed a little, but mostly they lived by hunting and fishing. This existence continued for a couple of years, until in 1818 both the Sparrows and Nancy Hanks Lincoln died of the milksick.* Some of the lifelong melancholy so much remarked upon by all who knew Abraham Lincoln might have taken hold that October day when the little boy sat in the dark forest, whittling pegs to fasten the rough planks of his mother's coffin.

A year later Tom Lincoln married a second time. The new wife was Sally Bush Johnston, a widow with three children, from Elizabethtown, Kentucky. The cabin still had a dirt floor when she arrived, almost three years after it had been built. She persuaded Tom Lincoln to lay a floor and to hang a door and some windows. She also gave the Lincoln children a new sense of maternal love and security. For example, she encouraged nine-year-old Abe to improve his ability to read and to write. She nursed him back to health when he was kicked in the head by a horse and was believed to be fatally injured.

The stepmother's encouragement of study at home was crucial because formal schooling was intermittent (Abe had less than a year's instruction in his entire life) and because Tom Lincoln was not interested in book learning for his children. He kept Abe at work doing the endless farm chores: attending to cattle, fixing fences, mending harnesses, hoeing, husking, and haying. As Abe grew into his teens, his skill with the ax earned a few dollars now and then as he was hired to cut trees and split rails. At night he stretched before the earth to read borrowed books and papers in the light of the fireplace.

* The milksick was a fever caused by drinking the milk of diseased cows.

At 19, Abe had an experience with Negroes that became a lifelong memory. On the way to New Orleans as a crewman on a flatboat, he and a companion were attacked by a gang of seven blacks bent on robbery. They drove off the robbers and got away, but Lincoln bore a permanent scar from a blow.

A year or so later, on another flatboat trip to New Orleans, Lincoln witnessed an auction of slaves. This left a scar deeper than the robber's blow. His cousin John Hanks recounted afterward that Abe was horrified by the sight of a pretty young mulatto girl being poked and pinched by prospective bidders. He recalled Abe's exclamation, "By God, boys, let's get away from this! If I ever get a chance at that thing, I'll hit it hard!" This sentiment reflects feelings he expressed all his life.

Another epidemic of the milksick scared old Tom Lincoln into moving to more hospitable territory. Illinois seemed the land of promise. On March 1, 1830, when Abraham was just 21, the family group, totaling 13, set out for Illinois. Abe drove one of the two ox teams on the two-week trek to a place 12 miles west of Decatur, Macon County, Illinois, on the north bank of the Sangamon River. On the way, he sold pins, needles, thread, and other "notions" to isolated settlers.

At the new home, Abe and John Hanks cleared a farm site and split enough locust and walnut rails—about 3,000—to fence ten acres. Then, chiefly because of the heavy snows of 1830–31, Tom Lincoln moved again, this time to Coles County, also in Illinois. Abe helped with this move too, but it marked his separation from the family unit. Now legally an adult at 21, he no longer owed his work and wages to his father.

After another flatboat trip to New Orleans as a hired hand for Denton Offutt, a merchant, Abe was put in charge of Offutt's store and mill at New Salem, a village overlooking the Sangamon River, near Springfield. This was in July, 1831.

Towering 6 feet, 4 inches and weighing about 190 pounds, Abe Lincoln was lithe and immensely strong. In a wrestling match arranged by Offutt, Lincoln defeated Jack Armstrong, the best rough-and-tumble fighter-wrestler in the area. This victory was important to Lincoln in two respects: it won the young stranger renown in a community that admired physical prowess, and it gained him the friendship and admiration of Armstrong, who, as the leader of a local faction, was a valuable ally in politics.

Lincoln was amiable, with a good word for everybody. He was such a fine storyteller that not only loafers, but also earnest, hardworking farmers and boatmen made it a point to stop at the store just to hear Abe spin yarns. He also was a helpful, accommodating youth, always willing to tote a box or a barrel or to lift a buggy out of the mud. In addition, he was so scrupulous in his dealings at the store that he became known as Honest Abe.

Moreover, he was a mystery, and this added to some people's interest in him. Sometimes he seemed sad. For a young fellow who liked to swap stories in a crowd, he spent a lot of time alone. Often he would sprawl in the shade on the bank of the Sangamon, fishing or reading or just thinking as he chewed a stem of grass.

Abe liked to read newspapers and to study whatever books he could get his hand on. One volume that he accidentally acquired helped to shape his life. In a barrel of odds and ends which he bought for 50 cents, he found

Blackstone's *Commentaries on the Laws of England*. After studying this book, he decided to become a lawyer.

When he was only 23, Abe was encouraged by friends to run for the legislature. In this very first race for office, he told the electorate his political philosophy, which never changed substantially:

> My politics are short and sweet, like the old woman's dance. I am in favor of a national bank. I am in favor of the internal improvement system and a high protective tariff. These are my sentiments and political principles. If elected, I shall be thankful; if not, it will be all the same.

Before the election, the Black Hawk War with the Indians broke out (1832), and Lincoln was among the first to volunteer. He was elected captain of the Sangamon company, an honor unusual for one so young and without military experience. He wrote in 1859 that his election as captain was "a success which gave more pleasure than any I have had since."

Back home from his brief military service, Lincoln had little time left to campaign for the legislature. Although he was not elected, he received 277 of the 300 votes cast in his own precinct. This was in spite of the fact that he was a Henry Clay Whig in a town that was strongly Andrew Jackson Democratic.

A variety of jobs carried Lincoln through the next few years. He was a surveyor's assistant, store owner who went bankrupt, postmaster, boatman, farmhand, woodcutter, and occasional pleader of minor cases before the justice of the peace, although not yet a lawyer. Moreover, the Sangamon County voters sent him to the legislature

Statue (now in Winchester, Illinois) by Leonard Crunelle of Abraham Lincoln as a volunteer soldier in the Black Hawk War (1832). *A U.S. Signal Corps photo, courtesy the National Archives.*

four successive times at two-year intervals, beginning in 1834, after the initial defeat in 1832.

In the legislature Lincoln quickly made a markedly favorable impression on his fellow Whigs. Evidence of this was the fact that he was chosen to manage Sangamon's successful effort to have Springfield made the capital. All of his eight Sangamon colleagues were older and more experienced than he; yet they chose him for this important leadership task. Further evidence of his recognition was that in two of his four terms in the legislature he was the Whigs' unanimous choice for Speaker, although he was beaten by the Democrats.

Like most of his fellow legislators, Lincoln believed that Illinois was on the verge of a great business boom, needing only public funds to prime it. He voted with the majority to pledge the state's credit for funds to promote railroads and canals and to make the rivers navigable. The legislation proved unsound fiscally, but Lincoln's record in this respect caused him no harm politically.

Lincoln's views on slavery first appeared on an official record in 1837 in a statement that he and one other legislator signed as a comment on antiabolition resolutions passed that year by the Illinois legislature. In Illinois mixed feelings about slavery grew out of the history of slavery in the state.

Illinois had come into the Union in 1818 as a free state, as part of the Northwest Territory designated free soil by the Ordinance of 1787. Nevertheless, there was strong proslavery sentiment in the southern part of the state. It was so virulent there that in 1837 the abolitionist editor Elijah Lovejoy was murdered by a proslavery mob in Alton, across the Mississippi from St. Louis, Missouri.

At the time feeling against abolitionism was so strong in the South that several states enacted laws making it a crime to speak or to write publicly against slavery. The Illinois legislature was one of many that enacted resolutions denouncing abolitionists. The Illinois resolutions expressed the sentiment of the legislature as (1) "highly disapproving" abolition societies, (2) holding that "the right of property in slaves is secured to the slave-holding states by the Constitution," and (3) declaring that "the general government cannot abolish slavery in the District of Columbia without the consent of the citizens of the said District, without a manifest breach of good faith."

Lincoln and a Sangamon County colleague, Dan Stone, issued the following as their formal comment on the resolution:

> Resolutions upon the subject of domestic slavery having passed both branches of the General Assembly at its present session, the undersigned hereby protest against the passage of the same.
>
> They believe that the institution of slavery is founded on both injustice and bad policy, but that the promulgation of abolition doctrines tends rather to increase than abate its evils.
>
> They believe that the Congress of the United States has the power, under the Constitution, to abolish slavery in the District of Columbia, but that the power ought not to be exercised, unless at the request of the people of the District.
>
> The difference between these opinions and those contained in the above resolutions is their reason for entering this protest.

Only Stone would join Lincoln in signing. Public

opinion in Sangamon County was "strongly averse to any discussion of the question of slavery." *

The language of the protest does not read like the philosophy of the Great Emancipator. Although Abraham Lincoln was opposed to the *institution* of slavery, he was not opposed to its legal continuation *within those states where it then was lawful*—in 1837 or in 1860.† The opinion that Lincoln consistently held until well into the Civil War was that slavery was an evil legally sanctioned in specified areas; that it should not be permitted to spread with legal approval; and that if confined to the then-existing slave states, it would be placed "where the public mind shall rest in the belief that it is in course of ultimate extinction," as he said in the "house divided" speech. He had no formula for ending slavery. However, in the Galesburg debate he expressed a principle that pointed to that goal. He said then that he believed slavery to be "a moral, social, and political evil" and that he hoped for a policy "that looks to the prevention of it as a wrong, and looks hopefully to the time when as a wrong it may come to an end."

When Lincoln moved to Springfield from New Salem in 1837, he was 28 years of age, a state legislator, a lawyer with no clients—and penniless. The failure of the New Salem grocery had left him with a debt that it took almost 15 years to pay off. He rode into Springfield on a borrowed horse. His only possessions were the clothes he wore, a change of linen, and a couple of law books.

---

* Nicolay and Hay, *Abraham Lincoln: A History* (New York: The Century Company, 1890), p. 151.
† In 1860 Lincoln wrote in an autobiographical sketch that the 1837 statement defined his position on slavery "and so far as it goes it was the same then that it is now."

Joshua Speed, a grocer to whom Lincoln applied for credit, was so moved by Lincoln's obvious melancholy and poverty that he offered him both credit and a free bed in a room above the store. Lincoln accepted and stayed for more than three years as Speed's guest.

Lincoln had been encouraged to move to Springfield by John T. Stuart, an older, successful lawyer. As a fellow legislator, Stuart, perceiving Lincoln's promising future, offered him a partnership in his Springfield law office. Stuart knew that an influential legislator like Lincoln could be an asset to a law office in the capital.

As a resident of Springfield, Lincoln soon found himself a frequent courtroom and legislative opponent of Stephen A. Douglas. The latter, although only 24 years old and four years Lincoln's junior, was popular socially and influential politically. On one stage or another, the flamboyant Douglas and the calm Lincoln crossed swords. They never were personal enemies, but they were professional rivals. Douglas made up for his failure to have Jacksonville made the capital by pushing through a bill to reform the state judiciary. He prevailed against the opposition of Lincoln and the rest of the Whigs. As a reward, he was appointed a state supreme court judge in 1841 when only 28 years old.

Douglas had got an early jump on Lincoln in the race for political and professional success.

3. The Little Giant Overshadows Lincoln

JOSHUA SPEED'S GROCERY store was the forum in which Stephen A. Douglas and Abraham Lincoln met in argument most often during their earliest years in public life. The store was a natural meeting place for the unattached young men of Springfield and for lawmakers from other towns when the legislature was not in session.

Speed and his lodger, Lincoln, were bachelors with time on their hands. So was Douglas. Although his residence was Jacksonville, Douglas spent a large part of his time in Springfield. In 1837, when Springfield became the capital and Lincoln moved there, Douglas was appointed secretary of the federal land office in Springfield. In the informal debates at the evening get-togethers in Speed's store, the young lawyers naturally argued opposing views.

As a Whig partisan and follower of Henry Clay, Lincoln favored high tariff rates, federal financing of an internal improvement program, and a national bank. Douglas, a convinced Democrat whose political idol was Andrew Jackson, argued otherwise.

23

Springfield at the time was a made-to-order forum for young politicians wishing to test their political theories and to polish their arguments. The new capital of Illinois was the home of politicians, officeholders, lobbyists, and lawyers representing the diverse forces at work within the state. Business was booming; Illinois' population was expanding; professional men were in demand. Douglas had come to Illinois from the East under the goad of ambition. Like Lincoln, he had come to Springfield because it was the best place for a young lawyer-politician to be.

As a boy whose physician father had died when he was an infant, Douglas had been almost as poor as Lincoln. However, his boyhood was spent in settled areas in Vermont and upper New York, where such schooling was available as Lincoln never knew. Douglas took advantage of these opportunities for education. In intervals of attending school, he worked as a cabinetmaker's apprentice in his native town of Brandon, Vermont (where he was born on April 23, 1813) and in Middlebury, Vermont. After attending Canandaigua Academy and reading law in Canandaigua, New York, he struck out on his own for the West.

Douglas was only 20 years old, ill, and with just 40 cents in his pocket when he reached Winchester, Illinois, which he had sought out because he had been told the town needed a school. With borrowed money he opened a school, read enough more law to get a license, and set up an office in the county seat, Jacksonville.

That was in 1834, when President Andrew Jackson was under attack by the Whigs for denying renewal of the charter of the national bank. Douglas arranged a countywide Democratic rally in support of Jackson. He gained immediate local fame with an eloquent defense of Old Hickory. He made so memorable an appearance that thereafter his supporters nicknamed him "the Little Gamecock" and "the Little Giant." He was only 5 feet, 2 inches tall, but gave the appearance of having a powerful physique.

Douglas soon took an important role in organizing the Democratic party in Illinois. His zeal and hard work won the favorable attention of party leaders. His first political reward was election to the legislature at the age of 23. There, in the 1836 session at Vandalia, he met for the first time Abraham Lincoln, the second-term Whig from New Salem.*

A rapid succession of important offices made Douglas a prominent young man. He was appointed chairman of the Democratic party, secretary of state of Illinois, and a state supreme court judge before his election to the national House of Representatives in 1843.

With a population of only 1,500 when it became the capital, Springfield nevertheless had a lively social life, in which Douglas was conspicuous. Several of the principal families were from the South, including Mr. and Mrs. Ninian Edwards. Mrs. Edwards's sister, Miss Mary Todd, of Louisville, Kentucky, was popular in the Springfield social set. She was a representative of the proslavery sentiment, which had strong support in some parts of free-soil Illinois.

The bachelor lawyers, Lincoln and Douglas, regularly were guests at the Springfield parties and dances. So was Mary Todd. One of the men's early rivalries was for the

---

* Lincoln described Douglas at that time as "the least man" in stature he had ever seen.

attention of the Kentucky belle. Contemporaries disagreed as to whether Douglas wished to marry her. In any event, she chose Lincoln for her husband. After a troubled courtship, they were married on November 4, 1842.

By that time Lincoln was a modestly successful lawyer, and Douglas was a state supreme court judge. Court was held at different times and in different towns. Lawyers who followed the court sittings from town to town were said to be "on the circuit." Lincoln at that time was on the circuit six months out of twelve.

Lincoln's career was influenced by life on the circuit. There he became acquainted with many of the most able lawyers and with other influential people in Illinois. He came to know the viewpoints of the people. On the sometimes lonely rides by buggy or horseback, he had the opportunity to reflect upon the political and social problems of the times. Most pressing of the problems was what, if anything, to do about slavery.

On the circuit Lincoln made a reputation as a good lawyer, a good Whig, a good friend—and a good story-teller. His stories were given added humor by Lincoln's droll delivery and his habit of giving them local settings. Usually, they illustrated a point he was making to a jury or in a political speech or to an impromptu court-day crowd. Such was the anecdote he told when expressing pleasure at being praised: "It reminds me of the boy I knew in Indiana who liked gingerbread better than anything, and reckoned he got less of it."

Like Douglas a hardworking party man, Lincoln became an acknowledged Whig leader by the early 1840s. Noting the Democrats' success under Douglas's disciplined organization, he insisted that the Whigs emulate the rival party.

Contrasted with the brilliant Douglas, who was given a succession of the plums of office in payment for his party work, Lincoln was little rewarded. His turn did come in 1846, when he put in a claim to be the Whig nominee for Congress. Given the nomination, Lincoln won the election against a Democratic rival who was a famous preacher, Peter Cartwright.

When Lincoln went to Washington in 1847 as the lone Whig member of Congress from Illinois, Stephen A. Douglas was just beginning his spectacular career as a United States senator. Already he had served two terms as a representative with such distinction that his fellow Democrats had elected him chairman of the territories committee in the House. Now he was elected chairman of the Senate territories committee. In 1847 Lincoln was an obscure member of the House, while at the same time Douglas was a man of national prominence. As Lincoln acknowledged (in 1854):

> Twenty-two years ago Judge Douglas and I first became acquainted. We were both young then; he a trifle younger than I. Even then, we were both ambitious; I, perhaps, quite as much as he. With me, the race of ambition has been a failure—a flat failure; with him it has been one of splendid success. His name fills the nation; and is not unknown, even, in foreign lands.

As members of different bodies of the Congress, Lincoln and Douglas did not come into direct dispute during Lincoln's one-term congressional career. However, their political differences were evidenced by their contrasting views on current issues.

Lincoln challenged the legality of the U.S. war on

Mexico, arguing that President Polk had started the bloodshed by killing Mexicans on Mexican soil. Douglas, on the other hand, believed the United States was in the right and strongly supported Polk.

Lincoln voted for the Wilmot Proviso, an attempt to enact a law to prohibit slavery in any territory acquired from Mexico. This was consistent with his stand that slavery should not be extended beyond its existing boundaries. Douglas, however, was not in favor of such a restriction.

In Washington, Lincoln again saw at first hand the workings of the slave trade. Then, the nation's capital was federally controlled. Under federal law, ownership of slaves was legal in Washington, and the city was a thriving center of trade in Negroes. Lincoln saw the slave pens from the windows of the Capitol. He described a "sort of Negro livery stable, where droves of Negroes were collected, temporarily kept, and finally taken to Southern markets, precisely like droves of horses." *

Lincoln consistently voted in support of the American troops in the Mexican war. However, his persistent efforts to embarrass the Democratic administration as to the justness of the war were unpopular in Illinois. His constituents largely supported the creed—*our country, may she ever be right; but our country, right or wrong!*

By the close of his two-year term, Lincoln was so unpopular at home that it was doubtful that he could be reelected. He took the advice of influential Whigs and did not try. Lincoln's district, the only Whig district in

* The Washington slave market was known as the Georgia Pit. Slave breeding was an important industry in adjacent Virginia, where in some years as many as 6,000 slaves were sold to the Southern market.

Illinois, went Democratic. The state also sent another Democrat, James Shields, to the Senate to join Stephen A. Douglas.

So, as 1848 drew to a close, it appeared that Lincoln's public career was ending also. He was an ex-officeholder with no apparent political prospects and only the sparse law practice that his partner William Herndon had held together during his absence in Washington.

At the same time Douglas continued his notable and much publicized career. Upon the chairman of the territories committee centered the pressures of national expansion and the problems of the place of slavery in the new lands. Douglas was in the eye of the public, the most conspicuous and potentially the most influential public figure. Party leaders were guided by him. The president sought his counsel. Not yet 36 years old, he was the ideal and the idol of young Democrats. As early as 1853 he was being spoken of as the party's nominee for president.

Back in Springfield, Lincoln settled into a kind of gloom. He made no political speeches. He started again the long circuit of the court sessions in eight counties. At age 40, Lincoln had not made much of a public mark. There was nothing in his prospects that promised any brighter future.

4. Lincoln Wakens

THE NATIONAL DIFFERENCES about slavery had existed from Revolutionary days. National policy about it was conceived in compromise. The Constitution of 1787 provided that importation of slaves and trade in slaves could not be prevented by Congress prior to 1808. The bargain that bought Southern ratification of the Constitution included the provision that three-fifths of a state's slaves should be counted in establishing that state's population for representation in Congress.

The second great compromise about slavery was the Missouri Compromise of 1820. This permitted Missouri to come into the Union as a slave state, provided that all other territory within the Louisiana Purchase north of 36 degrees 30 minutes should be free soil.

In 1850 new conditions gave the problem of slavery new urgency. When new land was acquired from Mexico in the South and Southwest, the status of slavery there was the primary source of dispute between the pro and antislavery factions.

While Lincoln plodded along in the obscurity of the

31

court circuit, Douglas held the spotlight in the drama of congressional debate about slavery in the new West. His leadership brought into being the Compromise of 1850.

The main elements of that compromise were as follows:

1. *For the North:* admission of California as a free state and abolition of the slave trade (but not of slave ownership) from the District of Columbia
2. *For the South:* the Fugitive-Slave Law requiring active assistance of Northerners in returning escaped slaves and a guarantee that New Mexico and Utah would be organized into territories with no prohibition of slavery.

Douglas was proud of his role in bringing about the Compromise of 1850. He thought that it affirmed "the right of the people to form and regulate their own internal concerns and domestic institutions in their own way." He felt that slavery would no longer be a sectional issue. So believing, he told the Senate on December 23, 1851, that he never again would speak in Congress about slavery.

Douglas was a strong candidate for the Democratic nomination for the presidency in the 1852 campaign. As late as the forty-eighth ballot in the national convention, he came close to winning; but finally a dark horse, Franklin Pierce of New Hampshire, was nominated.

Always a loyal party man, Douglas campaigned for Pierce, helping him to win the White House. But Douglas's friends, aggrieved that the Little Giant had been maneuvered out of the nomination, began immediately to work for his nomination in 1856. His place as a leader was

Stephen A. Douglas, the senator from Illinois, at about the time of the Lincoln-Douglas debates of 1858. *Courtesy the Library of Congress.*

strengthened by his unchallenged rule of the Democratic party in Illinois. He was elected to his second term as senator by a legislative vote of 75 to 20. He was the Northwest's leading man.

The need to organize the western lands into territories, which in due time would become states, now engrossed Douglas. It was his responsibility as chairman of the committee on territories to initiate and process the necessary legislation. Railroads were needed to connect the Pacific with the Middle West and to serve the westward advance of commerce. Formal governments were needed in the Indian-inhabited lands to encourage settlement and protect the railroads.

Douglas's task was made difficult by the politics of expansion. Until now the South had controlled the federal government. By exercise of political strength, the South had kept a balance between the free and the slave states. With equal representation in the Senate under the constitutional formula and by maintaining solidarity in the Senate, the South had effective control of the federal apparatus. At the least, the Southern Senate bloc could veto any legislation that it did not like.

Now—in the early 1850s—the South knew that the more rapid growth of population in the North portended a shift of the balance of power. For half a century the states had come into the Union as slave and free pairs.* The South had complete identity of interest on such sectional concerns as slavery, free trade (tariff policy), and acquisition of new lands in the West, in the Caribbean, and even in Central America. But unless slavery was permitted in enough newly admitted States to balance

* In 1854 they were even, at 15 each.

new free-soil states, even a united South soon would be
outnumbered in the Senate as well as in the House. The
Southern leaders believed that their vital sectional interests
were bound up in the policy of slavery extension and its
corollary of equal strength in the national government.

Many Southerners, like John C. Calhoun of South
Carolina, believed that the South could not remain in
the Union with safety unless sectional political balance
was preserved. They believed that unless abolitionist agitation ceased, the South would have to secede from the
Union, and could do so legally. The Compromise of
1850 had banked the fire of slavery agitation for a time
because of the moderate Southerners' belief that it upheld
"the principle of non-interference by Congress, the right
of the people to hold slaves in a common Territory." *

As a partisan Democrat, Stephen A. Douglas naturally
was an ally of the overwhelmingly Democratic South.
His first wife was the owner by inheritance of scores
of slaves. Douglas, however, refused a gift of a slave-stocked
plantation offered by his father-in-law. Douglas explained
that he did not wish to own that kind of property,
although he had no objection to others owning it.

Faced with the task of devising legislation that would
open the West, Douglas's first problem was to come up
with a formula about slavery that would satisfy every
section, or as nearly so as practicable. The formula that
he came up with was the Kansas-Nebraska Act.

It proved to be an unsuccessful formula, for it stirred
new agitation over slavery. Moreover, it wakened Abraham
Lincoln from his political torpor.

* Allen Johnson, *Life of Stephen A. Douglas* (New York: The Macmillan Company, 1908), p. 189.

5. The Kansas-Nebraska Act

THE KANSAS-NEBRASKA ACT WAS an attempt to resolve irreconcilable differences. One of the differences was constitutional. The Constitution specifically limited the area of slavery *—but it also promised equal protection of the laws to all citizens.** The latter meant that property (a slave) lawfully held in one place would equally be lawfully held when taken into any other place.

Another difference was moral. Slave owners generally felt that slave owning was right. Churchmen said it was a religious duty to give benighted blacks the blessings of Christianity denied them in Africa. Northerners generally believed that human bondage was wrong. Slave labor appeared to be a necessity in the cotton-tobacco economy

---

* Article I, Section 9: The migration or importation of such persons as any of the states now existing shall think proper to admit, shall not be prohibited by the Congress prior to the year one thousand eight hundred and eight, but a tax or duty may be imposed on such importation, not exceeding ten dollars for each person.
** Article IV, Section 2: The citizens of each state shall be entitled to all privileges and immunities of citizens in the several states.

of the South. It was not adaptable to the commercial-industrial North. These economic facts affected the moral outlook of both sections.

The most extreme antislavery people, the abolitionists, were for immediate action.

Douglas's formula was evolved in recognition of the fact that he could not ignore the claims of the slave owners that they had a right to take slaves to Kansas and Nebraska, nor could he ignore the demands of the Free-Soilers that the new lands should be free.

Douglas's solution was what he called "popular sovereignty." He said that it affirmed the right of slaveholders to take and to hold their human property in the twin territories of Kansas and Nebraska, just as was provided for the territories of Utah and New Mexico by the Compromise of 1850. However, he said, the doctrine of popular sovereignty also affirmed the right of the people of the territories to refuse to enact laws protecting slave ownership. This has been termed "the doctrine of unfriendly legislation."

In explaining the Kansas-Nebraska Bill to the Senate, Douglas said: *

We were aware that from 1820 to 1850, the abolition doctrine of Congressional interference with slavery in the territories and new states had so far prevailed as to keep up an incessant slavery agitation in Congress, and throughout the country, whenever any new territory was to be acquired or organized. We were also aware that in 1850 the right of the people to decide this question for themselves, subject only to the Constitution, was substituted

* U.S., Congress, Senate, *Report*, Appendix to *Congressional Globe*, 33d Cong., 1st sess., 4 January 1854, p. 326.

for the doctrine of Congressional intervention. The first question, therefore, which the committee were called upon to decide, and indeed, the only question of material importance in framing this bill, was this: Shall we adhere to and carry out the principle recognized by the Compromise Measures of 1850, or shall we go back to the old exploded doctrine of Congressional interference, as established in 1820, in a large portion of the country, and which it was the object of the Wilmot Proviso to give a universal application, not only to all the territory we then possessed, but all which we might hereafter acquire?

The committee report said the Compromise of 1850 was intended to have "a far more comprehensive and enduring effect than the mere adjustment of the difficulties arising out of the recent acquisition of Mexican Territory. They [the principles of the Compromise of 1850] were designed to establish certain great principles, which would not only furnish adequate remedies for existing evils, but in all time to come avoid the perils of a similar agitation, by withdrawing the question of slavery from the halls of Congress and the political arena, and committing it to the arbitrament of those who were immediately responsible for its consequences."

To assure Southern senators' support of the Nebraska Bill, as it came to be known, Douglas was persuaded to include express language nullifying the Missouri Compromise. Had he not done so, there was the probability that the proposed law would die as it had died in the previous Congress. Without a government in the Kansas-Nebraska Territory, there would be no railroad to the Pacific across that vast Indian-held area. Such a railroad was Stephen A. Douglas's goal. He was an expansionist.

He wanted the United States to be "an ocean-bound republic." To bind the Pacific to the East by rail was essential to this ambition. This was his goal as a statesman, and his duty as chairman of the territories committee. It was consistent with his personal interests as a Chicago and Wisconsin real estate speculator. A railroad to the West connecting with Chicago, perhaps with that city as the hub of a rail network, was desirable for Illinois. The voters of Illinois were Douglas's primary constituency.

The language of the final version of the Nebraska Bill was calculated to placate, if not to please, all factions. The bill as enacted asserted that it did not propose to legislate slavery into, or exclude it from, any state or territory, but was intended "to leave the people thereof perfectly free to form and regulate their domestic institutions in their own way, subject only to the Constitution of the United States."

Douglas's personal view was that the Nebraska Bill should not be objectionable to the North because, as a practical matter, the climate and soil of the region were not conducive to slavery. Despite vociferous opposition from abolitionists and more moderate antislavery forces, Douglas was able to get the bill enacted into law. President Franklin Pierce, who sympathized with the South, signed it into law on May 30, 1854.

Douglas believed that with popular sovereignty he had provided a solution to the slavery-extension question that was acceptable to everyone except the extremists of both sides. Events proved that, in fact, he had provided not peace, but a sword. He had created in the Nebraska Bill a situation in which the proslavery and the antislavery forces each began an immediate push to gain the voting majority in Kansas Territory. Kansas was the object of contention, rather than Nebraska, because Kansas bordered the slave state Missouri whereas Nebraska was bounded by free states or territories. Control of Kansas was an attainable goal for the slavery supporters. They sent men into Kansas from Missouri for the express purpose of voting or of intimidating antislavery settlers. The Missourians so employed were not settlers; they were incursionists making forays into Kansas and returning to their own soil. The epithet *Border Ruffians* was applied to them.

Determined not to lose Kansas for lack of effort, the abolitionists and their supporters financed the movement of free-soil sympathizers to the territory. The New England Emigrant Aid Society sent parties armed with rifles (Beecher's Bibles *) to colonize Kansas. The first bloodshed of the impending Civil War spilled onto the soil of Kansas. In fact, the territory came to be known as Bleeding Kansas.

Douglas also had created an atmosphere in which thoughtful citizens of the United States of all political persuasions now had reason to doubt the trustworthiness of their national government. For more than 30 years they had been led to believe that the Missouri Compromise assured that there never would be slavery in the Louisiana Purchase territory north of 36 degrees 30 minutes except in Missouri. Douglas himself as recently as 1849 had spoken approvingly of the Missouri Compromise. Lincoln quoted him as having said then, "all men and parties approved the Missouri Compromise,"

---

* *Beecher's Bibles* were rifles bought with funds contributed by the congregation of the Rev. Henry Ward Beecher.

Text of a speech of October 23, 1849, by Stephen A. Douglas at Springfield, Illinois, as reported in the *Illinois State Register* of November 3, 1849. In this speech, Douglas described the Missouri Compromise as having become "canonised in the hearts of the American people as a sacred thing . . ." *Courtesy the Library of Congress.*

and as having said, "All the evidences of public opinion" at that time "seemed to indicate that this compromise had become canonised in the hearts of the American people, as a sacred thing, which no ruthless hand would ever be reckless enough to disturb." * Now that Douglas's own Nebraska Bill superseded the Missouri Compromise, the slavery controversy was aflame again. Kansas and Nebraska were part of the Louisiana Purchase, yet Douglas's new law said in effect that whichever faction established a voting majority in a particular area could decide as to the existence of slavery there.

The outrage of the abolitionists over the Nebraska law brought on renewed agitation in New England for breaking up the Union. There had been strong secessionist sentiment at varying times and places in the North. Now if slavery extension were to be made lawful, Northern radicals wanted to pull out of a government that would condone it. Other Northerners were equally willing to let the slave states secede.

Some abolitionists believed that a nation that countenanced slavery was not worth preserving. Some radical Southerners felt the same way for a different reason: a government that promised equal protection of the laws to all citizens *except* as to slave ownership was, in their judgment, not worth preserving.

Another effect of the Kansas-Nebraska Act was that it brought Abraham Lincoln from his semiretirement from politics. He said of himself in his autobiographical sketch: "In 1854 his profession had almost superseded

---

* Reported by the *Illinois State Register*, Springfield, Ill., Nov. 3, 1849, as having been asserted by Douglas in a speech in Springfield, Oct. 23, 1849.

the thought of politics in his mind, when the repeal of the Missouri Compromise aroused him as he had never been before."

He made his first speech against the Nebraska Bill on August 26, 1854. It was made in behalf of the candidacy for reelection to Congress of Richard Yates, a Whig. Not having made the speech before, Lincoln went to the small town of Winchester, Illinois, "to try it on the dog" before delivering it to larger audiences.

The incident of the speech at Winchester is but another of the striking contrasts that mark the lives of Lincoln and Douglas. The Little Giant had tested his arguments for popular sovereignty in great debates with other famed and powerful leaders. His forum had been the Senate floor; the audience, the Congress of the United States and the press. He had prevailed and had seen the president put his signature to a law championed by Stephen A. Douglas. Lincoln's first tryout was in the sultry court-room in a prairie town before a few dozen prospective voters. Nothing of national importance depended upon the persuasiveness of Lincoln's words as had been the case with Douglas.

Or so it seemed.

6. The Warm-up for the Great Debates

WHEN CONGRESS ADJOURNED in 1854, Stephen Arnold Douglas had to return to Illinois to mend his political fences. Abolitionists and Free-Soilers were enraged by his sponsorship of the Nebraska Bill—so much so, he said later, that his way from Washington to Chicago was lighted by the burning of his effigy. Some newspapers called him "Benedict Arnold" Douglas. His leadership of the Democratic party in the state was not at issue, but the party's control of the state was threatened.

The stage thus was set for the Whigs and their successor party, the Republicans, to challenge the Democrats—and for Lincoln to face Douglas on the issue of slavery extension.

During the next four years Douglas and Lincoln tested and refined their arguments. They did not debate face-to-face during those years. Often, however, they addressed essentially the same Illinois crowds, sometimes on the same or successive days. Douglas spoke as the man responsible for the Nebraska Bill, as a national Democratic leader, and as an incumbent senator ambitious for the presidential nomination in 1856.

How did Lincoln become the chief spokesman for the opposition, the man to face the redoubtable Douglas on his favorite ground, the platform?

In the first place, Lincoln was the leading Whig in Illinois despite being out of office and having been out of the public eye since leaving Congress.

In the second place, Lincoln had prepared himself well for a new public role during the years of semiretirement. He had engaged in a course of self-improvement. This had included mastery of geometry, a system of logic adaptable to the practice of law. He had studied the profession of law instead of being satisfied with the mere courtroom conduct of cases.

In the third place, Lincoln had familiarized himself with the dilemma of slavery in the United States in all its aspects: historical, constitutional, statistical, legal. He was a subscriber to numerous newspapers and a close reader of them all—especially of their political and governmental news. His partner Herndon, an abolitionist zealot, subscribed to many magazines and purchased books on political and philosophical subjects, which he made available to Lincoln. The latter made notes on envelopes and pieces of paper, cut out clippings of newspaper reports on Douglas's Senate speeches and other pertinent material, and methodically assembled the data which helped him compose his speeches at the propitious time. When the time came to meet Douglas, Lincoln was familiar with Douglas's arguments and his forensic ploys as applied to the defense of the Nebraska Bill.

Lincoln's speeches in behalf of Richard Yates for

Congress attracted much favorable attention. Soon he was besieged with requests to speak on the Nebraska Bill either in direct opposition to Douglas or simply to encourage Free-Soilers in the belief of the rightness of their cause.

During the election campaign of 1854, it was suggested to Douglas that there would be great interest in "a joint discussion" between him and Lincoln. Douglas refused, saying, "No, I won't do it! I come to Chicago, and there I am met by an old-line Abolitionist; I come down to the center of the State, and I am met by an old-line Whig; I go to the South end of the State, and I am met by an anti-Administration Democrat. I can't hold the Abolitionist responsible for what the Whig says; I can't hold the Whig responsible for what the Abolitionist says, and I can't hold either responsible for what the Democrat says. It looks like dogging a man over the State. This is my meeting; the people have come to hear me, and I want to talk to them." *

The issue between Douglas and Lincoln became clear-cut in their speeches on successive days to crowds at the state fair in Springfield, October 3 and 4, 1854. Douglas spoke first, defending the Nebraska Bill. His argument was that the people of the entire country had equal interest and equal rights in any new territory. Thus, he said, the owner of hogs had a right to take his hogs there—and that each such owner was entitled to equal protection of the laws. He contended that the people of Kansas and Nebraska were capable of making their own judgments on domestic matters, including whether to permit slavery. The object of the Nebraska Bill, he said, was "neither to legis-

* James S. Ewing, quoted by Paul M. Angle in *The Lincoln Reader*, (Rutgers University Press, 1947), p. 205.

late slavery into a territory nor to exclude it therefrom, but to leave the people perfectly free to form and regulate their domestic institutions, in their own way, subject only to the Constitution of the United States."

The nub of Douglas's view was that Negroes were like other property and that the people of a territory had a right to admit or to exclude such property as they saw fit, just as they might admit or exclude liquor.

Lincoln, in his speech the next day, denied that human slaves and cattle were the same class of property. He said that even the South made a distinction between slaves and other property. He pointed out that the census of 1850 showed 434,239 free Negroes in the country along with 3,638,808 slaves. The current value of slaves was $500 apiece.

"How comes this vast amount of property to be running about without owners?" Lincoln asked. "We do not see free horses or free cattle running at large. How is this? All these free blacks are the descendants of slaves or have been slaves themselves; and they would be slaves now but for something which has operated on their white owners. What is that something? Is there any mistaking it? In all these cases it is your sense of justice and human sympathy continually telling you that the poor Negro has some natural right to himself. . ."

Then, and in a speech in Peoria, Illinois, October 16, 1854, Lincoln reminded his listeners that the Nebraska Bill had caused bloodshed in Kansas between proslavery and antislavery factions. The goal was control of the territorial government and of the constitutional convention. Lincoln said that the Missouri Compromise ought to be restored to prevent such strife in other territories. Otherwise, he said, "the South would be flushed with triumph and tempted to excess; the North, betrayed as they believe, brooding on wrong and burning for revenge. One side will provoke; the other resent."

The anti-Nebraska partisans unexpectedly won a majority of the seats in the Illinois legislature in the election of 1854. Lincoln's role as chief spokesman against Douglas and principal advocate of the Missouri Compromise restoration made him the acknowledged Whig leader of the state. He sought the reward of election to the United States Senate. In the vote in the legislature on February 8, 1855, Lincoln received 44 votes on the first ballot; 50 would have elected him. It became evident that if he remained in the contest, a pro-Nebraska Bill man would be elected, so he threw his support to Lyman Trumbull. Trumbull had left the Democratic party in protest against the Nebraska law. Lincoln's support elected him, although he had not formally become a Whig.*

By May 29, 1856, when the Republican party in Illinois was organized at Bloomington, Lincoln's views on slavery had been fully developed and expressed. He opposed the extension of slavery into territory where it did not then legally exist. He believed that making new territories subject to the *possibility* of slavery almost certainly meant extension of it. He believed that restoration of the Missouri Compromise was essential to contain slavery and to prevent elsewhere the violence that had given Bleeding Kansas its name.

* Trumbull later became a Republican.

7. "A House Divided Cannot Stand"

NORMALLY, THE 1858 SENATORIAL campaign in Illinois would have been strictly a two-party contest, with the incumbent Douglas as the Democratic nominee for re-election and the challenging Lincoln the choice of the new and hopeful Republican party. However, in 1858 the contest was not a clear-cut, two-party race because Douglas was opposed by the Democrats' national leadership. This opposition was headed by President James Buchanan. The president was counseled by a small group of Southern political leaders who exercised controlling influence on him. They distrusted Douglas. They did not want him to be the Democratic nominee for president in 1860 because he might be more amenable to the sentiment of the anti-slavery Northern Democrats than to the proslavery Southern Democrats. The first effect of the president's declared opposition was a minor splintering-off of Douglas's Democratic support in Illinois. These pro-Buchanan Illinois Democrats, called "Danites," * were anti-Douglas, loyal to

* The Danites were a militant Mormon sect then living in Illinois.

Buchanan in principle, or hopeful of patronage, or all three.

The president's opposition to Douglas was the bitter fruit that Douglas harvested from his own planting—the Kansas-Nebraska legislation. The proslavery constitutional convention had drawn up a charter for Kansas, which would legalize slavery in the territory. Rather than permit a popular vote on the entire constitution, the proslavery convention provided that the people could vote *only* on the clause permitting slavery. It was further provided that *even if the slave clause was rejected, the slaves already in Kansas would continue to be slaves lawfully held in Kansas.* This was known as the Lecompton Constitution. President Buchanan supported it because his Southern advisors favored it.

The Lecompton Constitution's provision that existing slavery could continue even if the proslavery clause was voted down was incompatible with Douglas's concept. To him, popular sovereignty meant that a majority of the voters of Kansas could vote for or against slavery as a legal institution in their state and that the majority's will would prevail. The Lecompton Constitution provided no such choice. Even if the majority voted against the slave clause, those who were slaves in Kansas at the time of the vote would continue to be slaves after the vote.

Douglas was uncompromisingly and outspokenly opposed to the Lecompton "heads I win, tails you lose" formula. He made a personal appeal in the White House to Buchanan that the president repudiate Lecompton. Upon Buchanan's refusal to do so, Douglas announced publicly his breach with the administration on that issue. The Illinois senator considered the matter simply as a difference on that issue alone—serious but not a cause for an irreconcilable break between him and the Democratic party regulars. Buchanan felt otherwise. To him, Douglas no longer was a loyal Democrat and should be defeated. He instituted a program of dismissal from office of postmasters, marshals, and other jobholders who were in public office by grace of Douglas's patronage. He sent henchmen into Illinois to foment party opposition to the Little Giant. His goal was to bring about the election of a sufficient number of legislators to elect as senator a Democrat other than Douglas—one who would vote to Buchanan's liking.

Because of his much publicized opposition to the Lecompton Constitution, Douglas regained favor with some of the Northern Democrats who had turned away from him because of his authorship of the Nebraska Bill. Some Republicans and some antislavery movements, such as the Abolitionist party, favored reelection of Douglas. Indeed, there was considerable sentiment to persuade the Republican party in Illinois to "adopt" Douglas as the Republican senatorial choice in 1858.

Lincoln successfully opposed the proposal that the Republican party embrace Douglas. His opposition was based on three points. First, he was ambitious personally and unwilling to share his Republican leadership with Douglas. He believed that there was a reasonable chance that he could defeat Douglas for the Senate. Second, he believed that the new Republican party would compromise its identity and its independence if it adopted Douglas as its standard-bearer. Third, he had no reason to believe that Douglas would adopt Republican party principles. He recognized that to have the party join Douglas, rather than have Douglas join the party, offered nothing of permanent value to the Republicans of Illinois.

Douglas successfully sought the continued support of

the old-line Democrats in Illinois. He welcomed also the support of anyone else who opposed the Lecompton Constitution. Lincoln kept the Illinois Republican party organization from supporting Douglas formally, but part of his task in the 1858 campaign was to keep the rank-and-file Republican voters in line.

Lincoln by 1858 was the unchallenged choice of the Illinois Republican party to oppose Douglas. No other candidacy for the party's nomination to succeed Douglas got off the ground. The nominating convention in Springfield on June 16 acted promptly to emphasize Lincoln's leadership. Its initial action was to pass unanimously a resolution reading: "Resolved, That Abraham Lincoln is the first and only choice of the Republicans of Illinois for the United States Senate, as the successor to Stephen A. Douglas."

The nomination put Lincoln directly in the national spotlight for the first time in his career. Buchanan's intervention against Douglas focused the country's attention on the Illinois election campaign. Lincoln had known for weeks that he would be the Republican nominee. County and sectional meetings preparatory to the state convention had made this evident. He had worked on his acceptance speech long before the nomination. He had jotted memoranda on such bits of paper as were at hand, "filing" such notes in his tall hat. He had also pondered the Kansas situation and the slavery extension threat as he traveled the judicial circuit. In addition, he had put his thoughts into a carefully phrased speech, polished and refined by frequent alteration, and had read the final draft to political friends, asking their opinion. Almost unanimously, those friends and advisers opposed the introductory language of

*The speech, immediately succeeding,
was delivered, June 16. 1858 at Springfield Illinois, at the close of the
Republican State convention held
at that time and place, and by
which convention Mr. Lincoln
had been named as their candidate for U. S. Senator.*

Senator Douglas was not present.

Reference in Abraham Lincoln's handwriting (in a scrapbook
that he kept) to his "house divided" speech, which was given
in Springfield, Illinois, in acceptance of the Republican nomination for U.S. senator in the 1858 campaign against Stephen
A. Douglas. *Courtesy the Library of Congress.*

the speech, the language expressing the thought that has caused it to be known to history as the "house divided" speech. The doubters believed that the speech might be interpreted as Lincoln's endorsement of war, if necessary, to rid the country of slavery. Lincoln was not persuaded by the fears of the skeptics. He had decided that the time had come for the people to face up to what he believed to be the truth. So, in the opening paragraph of his speech of June 16, 1858, accepting the Republican senatorial nomination, Lincoln said:

> If we could first know where we are, and whither we are tending, we could better judge what to do, and how to do it. We are now far into the fifth year since a policy was initiated with the avowed object and confident prom-ise of putting an end to slavery agitation. Under the operation of that policy, that agitation has not only not ceased, but has constantly augmented. In my opinion, it will not cease until a crisis shall have been reached and passed. 'A house divided against itself cannot stand.' * I believe this government cannot endure permanently half slave and half free. I do not expect the Union to be dis-solved—I do not expect the house to fall—but I do expect it will cease to be divided. It will become all one thing, or all the other.

He went on to explain:

> Either the opponents of slavery will arrest the further spread of it, and place it where the public mind shall rest in the belief that it is in the course of ultimate ex-tinction; or its advocates will push it forward till it shall become alike lawful in all the states, old as well as new, North as well as South.

* Mark 3:25.

Douglas seized the first opportunity to make a campaign issue of the "house divided" speech. Upon arrival in Chicago from Washington on July 9, 1858, to open his election campaign, he told the crowd of thousands who greeted him:

> Mr. Lincoln advocated boldly and clearly a war of sections, a war of the North against the South, of the free states against the slave states—a war of extermination— to be continued relentlessly until the one or the other shall be subdued, and all the states shall either become free or become slave.

Douglas knew from long experience that Lincoln would be hard to beat. He had told a Washington editor, "I shall have my hands full. Lincoln is the strong man of his party, the best stump speaker in the West." In the Chicago speech of July 9, at which Lincoln was present, Douglas described him as "an honorable opponent," and as "a kind, amiable, and intelligent gentleman."

Throughout the campaign the rivals differed in their interpretations of what Lincoln meant by the "house divided" speech. Douglas reiterated that Lincoln advocated war over slavery. Lincoln insisted that he was not advocating any particular policy in that speech, that he was merely stating a fact. "I did not express my wish on anything," he said. "I simply expressed my expectation. Cannot Judge Douglas perceive a distinction between a purpose and an expectation? I have often expressed an expectation to die, but I have never expressed a wish to die."

As became evident later in the campaign, Lincoln used the "house divided" language as a shock tactic, an attention getter. He used a universally understood metaphor to alert his audience to a danger that they might not perceive. He believed that the repeal of the Missouri Compromise was part of a scheme to spread legalized slavery. Once established in a territory, slavery could take permanent root there. The way would be prepared for its acceptance elsewhere—in other territories, perhaps even other states.

The speech was a call to public opinion to be on guard. Lincoln had employed the "house divided" allusion in a speech in 1856 in Bloomington, Illinois, but its use had so alarmed his political advisers that he had promised them that he would not use it again in the 1856 campaign. Now, however, in 1858, Lincoln believed the time had come to say it again, as the sounding of an alarm. Again his advisers criticized him for the language, but this time he replied, "If I had to draw a pen across my record and erase my whole life from sight, and I had one poor gift or choice left as to what I should save from the wreck, I should choose that speech and leave it to the world unerased." *

Now began an arduous speaking schedule for both candidates. Douglas had the disadvantage of having to fight two foes: the Republicans led by Lincoln and his own Democratic party's national leadership. On the positive side for Douglas was the loyal support of most of the Illinois Democratic party leaders and the enthusiastic support of the state's younger rank-and-file Democrats. He never lost his appeal to the great majority of Illinois Democrats. As President Buchanan learned, even the enmity of the president and the energetic opposition to Douglas of

* Reported by Herndon (vol. 1, p. 70) as having been stated by Lincoln in June, 1858.

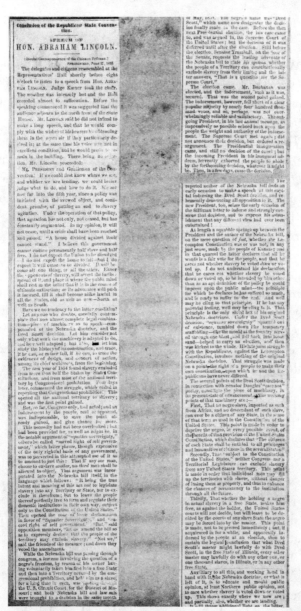

The first published report of Abraham Lincoln's "house divided" speech of June 16, 1858, as recorded in *The Chicago Tribune. Courtesy of Library of Congress.*

the White House managers could not damage Douglas in the estimation of his own people. He even had the sympathy appeal of an underdog because of presidential opposition.

Douglas and his managers arranged a schedule that had the Little Giant speaking every day except Sunday, sometimes two or three times. As Douglas's stump schedule was made public, the Republicans arranged for Lincoln to follow him closely—closely enough so that sometimes Lincoln could speak in the evening to an audience Douglas had addressed in the afternoon. This drew the Democratic charge that Lincoln could not attract a sizable audience on his own and was feeding on Douglas's ability to draw a crowd. Lincoln's managers were sensitive to this charge. They were aware, too, that the best way to bring the issues before the largest audiences was to have the candidates debate them. Lincoln agreed to challenge Douglas, which he did in a letter delivered to the senator on July 24.

Douglas accepted, reluctantly. There was no advantage to him in such joint discussions.

"Between you and me," he told his aides, "I do not feel that I want to go into this debate. The whole country knows me and has me measured. Lincoln, as regards myself, is comparatively unknown, and if he gets the best of this debate—and I want to say he is the ablest man the Republicans have got—I shall lose everything. Should I win, I shall gain but little." *

Although he further protested that the challenge was belated, after *his* speaking schedule had been made, Douglas accepted. He proposed that there be seven de-

---

* F. E. Stevens, "The Life of Stephen A. Douglas," in *Journal of the Illinois State Historical Society*, No. 16 (1923), p. 553.

Bement, Piatt Co. Ill,
July 30ᵗʰ, 1858

Dear Sir,

Your letter, dated yesterday, accepting my proposition for a joint discussion at one prominent point in each Congressional district as stated in my previous letter was received this morning.

The times and places designated are as follows:

Ottawa, Lasalle Co, August 21ˢᵗ, 1858
Freeport, Stevenson Co. " 27ᵗʰ "
Jonesboro, Union Co. September 15. "
Charleston, Coles Co. " 18 " "
Galesburg, Knox Co. October 7 " "
Quincy, Adams Co. " 13 " "
Alton, Madison Co. " 15, "

I agree to your suggestion that we shall alternately open and close the discussion. I will speak at Ottawa one hour, you can reply occupying an hour and a half and I will then follow for half an hour. At Freeport you shall open the discussion and speak one hour, I will follow for an hour and a half and you can then reply for

half an hour. We will alternate in like manner at each succeeding place.

Very resp'y
Yr ob't Serv't,
S. A. Douglas

Hon. A. Lincoln,
Springfield,
Ills.

Letter, dated July 30, 1858, from Stephen A. Douglas to Abraham Lincoln, setting forth the dates and places of the seven "joint discussions" as candidates for the office of U.S. senator. Reproduced from the collections of the Library of Congress.

bates, in different Congressional districts. He also proposed the format that he would open the first debate by speaking for one hour, that Lincoln would follow with a one-and-a-half-hour discussion, and that Douglas would conclude with a half-hour rebuttal. They would alternate as opening speakers. Lincoln agreed, although complaining that "by the terms . . . you take four openings and closes to my three." He had challenged; Douglas had accepted and had set the terms. Did he expect Douglas to allow *him* four openings and closes in the seven Congressional districts? Lincoln was not an admirer of Douglas. Perhaps his rather ungracious comment betrayed his feeling about his opponent.

The places and dates agreed upon for the debates were:

1. Ottawa, August 21
2. Freeport, August 27
3. Jonesboro, September 15
4. Charleston, September 18
5. Galesburg, October 7
6. Quincy, October 13
7. Alton, October 15.

The election would be held November 2. Lincoln and Douglas actually were campaigning in behalf of candidates for the Illinois legislature. The new legislature elected in November would, in January, choose between Douglas and Lincoln for United States senator. All members of the lower house were to be elected. Only half the Senate seats were at stake and most of the holdover senators were Democrats favoring Douglas.*

* The Seventeenth Amendment, in 1913, provided for popular vote for U.S. senator.

Even before announcement of the forthcoming debates, national interest in the campaign had been aroused. Major newspapers around the country arranged to send correspondents to report the speeches or to receive reports. For the first time in American history, political speeches were recorded verbatim by means of the newly devised shorthand. What each man said to the thousands who heard him was reported to the newspapers for millions to read. Stenographic reporting and the telegraph gave the country the opportunity, for the first time, to "sit in" on a major campaign.

The Lincoln-Douglas canvass was the first at which the national electorate was enabled to read and to ponder the latest developments right up to voting day. The national interest in the 1858 Illinois race was especially intense for a reason outside the immediate controversy over the Nebraska Bill. The reason was that Douglas was a front-runner for the Democratic presidential nomination in 1860. President Buchanan had let it be known that he would not seek the nomination. Douglas was in the forefront of those being talked of for the succession.

Very few thought of Lincoln as a presidential possibility. There was nothing in his record to match Douglas's glittering career. The only national attention he had received was when he had won 110 votes for the vice-presidential nomination in the 1856 Republican convention, which chose Fremont as its presidential candidate.

The newsmen who reported the 1858 campaign were keenly interested in describing for their readers the contrasts in appearance, debating style, and conduct of the rivals. The men were so different in so many ways that the reporters were able to give human interest to their accounts of the cut-and-dried political arguments. The papers mostly were very partisan. As was the common journalistic practice of the day, the reporters tended to reflect their papers' prejudices.

8. The Great Debates

THE LINCOLN-DOUGLAS DEBATES of 1858 were the climactic event of a classic political contest. They were the culmination of a long buildup. The national agitation over slavery had been building for decades. The last period of relative relaxation of the tensions had been for a brief four years following the Compromise of 1850. Since the repeal in 1854 of the Missouri Compromise, sectional antagonisms over slavery had reached the point which had prompted Lincoln's "house divided" analogy.

The rivalry of Lincoln and Douglas, like the nation's division over slavery, had been continuous over a long period. In 1852, 1854, and 1856 they had argued politics and policy on the stumps of Illinois. In this 1858 campaign they had discussed the issues in enough places and enough times to have built up public interest in the main event. The names of Stephen A. Douglas and Abraham Lincoln and what they stood for had been reported in newspapers and discussed in homes, churches, taverns and over fence rails for years. Each man had a large and loyal following.

Each was recognized by friends and foes as a capable speaker, in substance as well as style. Though their styles were markedly different, each was able to gain and to hold the attention of thousands of people out of doors with nothing to amplify his voice.

Douglas was very short, deep-chested, large-headed, well groomed, and poised and the possessor of an orator's baritone. He had an aggressive attack and a tongue's-tip familiarity with legislative history, which he used to good effect. He had had plenty of practice in the United States Senate.

Lincoln, tall, rawboned, in ill-tailored clothes, shambled to the platform and, at the beginning of his speeches at least, often appeared ill at ease. His voice was high-pitched, with a penetrating timbre. His manner toward his audience was one of explanation rather than declamation.

His prose style has been described thus: ". . . disciplined by the court room, made pungent by familiarity with plain people, stimulated by constant reading of Shakespeare, and chastened by study of the Bible" and ". . . that method of using words which was based on an arduous study of Blackstone, Shakespeare, and Isaiah." *

The speakers met in the first debate on August 21 in Ottawa. A railroad and canal town in north central Illinois, Ottawa had a permanent population of about 6,000. The debate in the public square attracted about 12,000. Hundreds of outsiders had camped the previous night on the edge of town. The rest had come into town during the morning by all kinds of conveyances, including oxcarts. By noon a thin haze of dust, raised by the thou-

* N. W. Stephenson, *Abraham Lincoln and the Union* (New Haven: Yale University Press, 1918), p. 54.

sands of feet and hooves, hung over the town. With no arranged seating for the audience, many assured themselves of some comfort by driving their carriages or wagons close to the speakers' platform and sitting in them during the speeches. Others scaled the posts supporting the roof of the newly carpentered speakers' platform, only to break the thin planks and fall on the heads of the reception committee.

As the lead-off speaker, the self-confident Douglas at once took the offensive by implying that Lincoln was an abolitionist. He claimed that Lincoln had connived to break up the old Whig and Democratic parties in Illinois in 1854 and had tried to unify the dissidents into the new so-called Black Republican party dedicated to abolitionist principles. These tenets had been adopted in a series of resolutions by one wing of the emerging Illinois Republican party. The resolutions had not become official party doctrine, however. Douglas asked Lincoln if he "still adhered" to those 1854 Republican doctrines.

This was the first of the questions exchanged by the rivals during the debates, and it set the precedent for Lincoln to use the same tactic in posing what became known as the Freeport Question in the second debate. Douglas's purpose was to try to make Lincoln admit that he was an abolitionist. If he could make the Illinois voters believe that Lincoln was in accord with the abolitionist demand for immediate emancipation, he would have scored a probably decisive point. Predominant Illinois sentiment in 1858 was anti-Negro.

Douglas at Ottawa reiterated that Lincoln fomented civil war in the "house divided" speech. The basic theme of Douglas's Ottawa speech was that popular sovereignty provided the logical solution to the slavery problem in the American political tradition. Let the people of a territory decide for themselves whether that territory should have or should not have slavery. He argued that no matter what Congress did or what the Supreme Court ruled, the people of a territory would decide slavery's status there by enacting or failing to enact the laws safeguarding property in slaves. Local attitudes would be decisive, and rightfully so, irrespective of national policy, Douglas asserted.

With characteristic caution, Lincoln did not answer specifically at Ottawa the seven questions that Douglas posed there. He made a general denial of the charge that he was an abolitionist and reserved the right to give specific answers in the next debate a week later. He knew that off-the-cuff answers possibly could give rise to real or pretended misunderstanding of his position. Misunderstanding could distort, and distortion could be damaging. Lincoln always tried to use language that would convey to the hearer precisely what Lincoln wanted him to understand. His associates have testified that habitually he examined the phrasing of his speeches to assure accurate understanding. His caution in delaying his reply to Douglas on the Ottawa platform was consistent with this practice.

At Ottawa, Lincoln made a serious accusation. He cited circumstantial evidence that he said pointed to a conspiracy between Presidents Pierce and Buchanan, Chief Justice Taney, and Senator Douglas to extend the boundaries of legal slavery. He claimed that this seeming evidence "proved" that the four had connived to bring forth the Supreme Court's Dred Scott case ruling that the Missouri Compromise was invalid. This, said Lincoln, was done in order to pave the way for public acceptance of the Kansas-Nebraska Bill as lawful. As evidence of the plot, he cited specific acts and statements of the presidents and of Douglas that the Scott decision "fitted," and that he said demonstrated concert among the four in advance of the decision. He deduced a conspiracy from acts that, in his opinion, fitted his conspiracy theory. He likened these acts to the construction of a building by carpenters working from a blueprint. He dramatized the "scare" feature of his charge by saying that so far the only missing element of betrayal of national trust was a Supreme Court ruling making slavery lawful everywhere—in *all* the states. He said the "blueprint" provided for that part of the slavery edifice in due time.*

Douglas denied the accusation. He had ignored it when Lincoln first made it in an earlier speech. Now he protested that it was so preposterous that he believed Lincoln could not be serious in making it.

Lincoln repeated the conspiracy accusation in the later debates, but he did not stress it because it never caught hold with the public as being true. Douglas called it "an infamous lie," denied having talked with either president about the Dred Scott case, and said that he had no intimation of what the decision would be.

The fundamental difference between Douglas and Lincoln on slavery was spelled out at Ottawa. That was the moral issue. Lincoln made it evident that he thought slavery was wrong both personally and as national policy.

---

* President Buchanan was told by a Supreme Court justice what the Dred Scott decision would be, in time for him to speak of it accurately in his inaugural address. However, there is no evidence that Douglas was aware of the nature of the forthcoming ruling or of Buchanan's secret knowledge. The decision, published Mar. 6, 1857, is reported in Howard Supreme Court Reports, Vol. 19, p. 393.

Douglas made it equally clear that he did not care whether slavery was or was not permitted to exist in a given political entity *as long as the white people there made the decision in a lawful way.* To put it more simply: Lincoln thought slavery was wrong; Douglas did not.

Douglas literally meant it when he said he did not care whether slavery "was voted down or voted up." Therefore, he had no objection to the expansion of slavery to all the new territories and perhaps the older ones, as long as his popular sovereignty doctrine was the rule of action. He had no scruples of conscience against human bondage. He believed that Negroes were inferior beings, not deserving of equal treatment with whites. His view was that the United States government was established for white people only. He said that he believed that the assertion of the Declaration of Independence that "all men are created equal" was not meant to apply to Negroes; that, in fact, it was meant to apply only to the white colonial Americans of 1776 relative to other English subjects who had remained in the British Isles.

Lincoln believed slavery to be evil. He said so many times, publicly and privately. He expressed his feeling most vividly in a letter of August 24, 1855, to his friend Joshua Speed, the storekeeper with whom Lincoln lived during his first three years in Springfield. He wrote:

> In 1841 you and I had together a tedious low-water trip on a steamboat from Louisville to St. Louis. You may remember, as I well do, that from Louisville to the mouth of the Ohio there were on board ten or a dozen slaves shackled together with irons. That sight was a continued torment to me, and I see something like it every time I touch the Ohio or any other slave border. It is not fair

for you to assume that I have no interest in a thing which has, and continually exercises, the power of making me miserable. You ought rather to appreciate how much the great body of the Northern people do crucify their feelings, in order to maintain their loyalty to the Constitution and the Union.

Lincoln also believed that the plight of the Negro in America was growing worse. "So far as peaceful voluntary emancipation is concerned," he said, "the condition of the Negro slave in America . . . is now as fixed and hopeless of change for the better, as that of the lost souls of the finally impenitent."

Lincoln also asserted another facet of true popular sovereignty doctrine that Douglas did not concede. He argued that *all* the people of the nation had a stake in what happened in a new territory. Douglas's doctrine was that the affairs of a new territory were its people's to deal with exclusively "subject only to the Constitution of the United States." Lincoln distinguished between the sovereignty of the states and the nonsovereignty of the territories.

Lincoln's moral view as to slavery did not extend to belief in full civil and social equality of Negroes with whites. He limited his declaration of equality for the Negro to "the right to put into his mouth the bread that his hands have earned." He was put on the defensive by Douglas's oft-repeated declarations that Lincoln advocated social and political equality of the Negro with the white. Several times and at considerable length Lincoln denied that this was true. At Ottawa he twice used the word *nigger*. At Charleston, in slavery-oriented Coles County, he gave his views explicitly:

. . . I am not, or ever have been, in favor of bringing about in any way the social and political equality of the white and black races—that I am not, nor have been, in favor of making voters or jurors of Negroes, nor of qualifying them to hold office, nor to inter-marry with white people; and I say in addition to this that there is a physical difference between the white and black races which I believe will forever forbid the two races living together on terms of social and political equality. And inasmuch as they cannot so live, while they do remain together there must be the position of superior and inferior, and I as much as any other man am in favor of having the superior position assigned to the white race. I say upon this occasion I do not perceive that because the white man is to have the superior position the Negro should be denied everything. I do not understand that because I do not want a Negro woman for a slave I must necessarily want her for a wife. My understanding is that I can just let her alone. I will add to this that I have never seen, to my knowledge, a man, woman, or child who was in favor of producing a perfect equality, social and political, between Negroes and white men.

Douglas was equally explicit. At Ottawa he said:

Mr. Lincoln reads from the Declaration of Independence, that all men are created equal, and then asks, how can you deprive a Negro of that equality which God and the Declaration of Independence award to him? He and they maintain that Negro equality is guaranteed by the laws of God, and that it is asserted in the Declaration of Independence. If they think so, of course they have a right to say so; and so vote. I do not question Mr. Lincoln's conscientious belief that the Negro was made his equal, and hence is his brother; but for my own part, I do not regard the Negro as my equal, and positively deny that he is my brother or any kin whatever. [Lincoln] holds that

the Negro was born his equal and yours, and that he was
endowed with equality by the Almighty, and that no
human law can deprive him of these rights which were
guaranteed to him by the Supreme Ruler of the Universe.
Now, I do not believe that the Almighty ever intended the
Negro to be the equal of the white man. If he did, he has
been a long time demonstrating the fact. For thousands
of years the Negro has been a race upon the earth, and
during all that time, in all latitudes and climates, wherever he has wandered or been taken, he has been inferior
to the race which he has there met. He belongs to an inferior race, and must always occupy an inferior position.
I do not hold that because the Negro is our inferior that
therefore he ought to be a slave. By no means can such a
conclusion be drawn from what I have said. On the contrary, I hold that humanity and Christianity both require
that the Negro shall have and enjoy every right, every
privilege, and every immunity consistent with the safety
of the society in which he lives. On that point, I presume,
there can be no diversity of opinion. You and I are bound
to extend to our inferior and dependent beings every right,
every privilege, every facility and immunity consistent
with the public good. The question then arises, what rights
and privileges are consistent with the public good. This is
a question which each State and Territory must decide for
itself—Illinois has decided it for herself. We have provided
that the Negro shall not be a slave, and we have also
provided that he shall not be a citizen, but protect him in
his civil rights, in his life, his person and his property,
only depriving him of all political rights whatsoever, and
refusing to put him on an equality with the white man.
That policy of Illinois is satisfactory to the Democratic
party and to me, and if it were to the Republicans, there
would be no question upon the subject; but the Republicans say that he ought to be made a citizen, and when
he becomes a citizen he becomes your equal, with all your
rights and privileges.

And at Ottawa Douglas said also:

> I believe this government was made on the white basis. I believe it was made by white men for the benefit of white men and their posterity forever, and I am in favor of confining citizenship to white men, of European birth and descent, instead of conferring it upon Negroes, Indians, and other inferior races.

The Ottawa debate's particular significance was to make apparent that there was a single major difference between the two candidates and that was as to the *rightness* or *wrongness* of slavery. Their differences on poir.s of governmental policy actually were logical consequences of their opposite views on the morality of slavery. On the other hand, they were like-minded in their desire to preserve the Union. Lincoln did not propose to interfere with slavery in the states where it then existed. He had no plan nor any time limit for ending it. Both men were agreed in opposition to the Lecompton Constitution, but their reasons for agreeing pointed to their differences over slavery. Douglas opposed Lecompton because it did not provide for a popular vote on the state's constitution as a whole. Lincoln opposed it because, he said, it provided that the people could vote to *admit* slavery to Kansas, but could not vote to *bar* slavery. Douglas interpreted popular sovereignty as permitting slavery if a majority of the territorial inhabitants wished it. Lincoln interpreted popular sovereignty as to the slavery question as a perversion of the right of self-government, with the effect "that if any one man choose to enslave another, no third man shall be allowed to object."

In the matter of tactics, Douglas perhaps "won" the

Ottawa debate. He took the offensive in that he implied that Lincoln previously had subscribed to abolitionism, and Douglas demanded to know if he had changed his principles. He charged that Lincoln wanted to make Negroes equal in all respects to whites. He claimed Lincoln had helped destroy the Whig party in Illinois. Lincoln thus basically was on the defensive in the Ottawa speech. He did not then reply to Douglas's charge of radical abolitionism, but he did deny that he had conspired to break up the Whig party, and he explained at length—as he felt he must, to an Illinois audience—that he did not favor equality of all rights for Negroes.

Lincoln took the offensive in making the charge of Democratic conspiracy to extend slavery. His main thrust, the one that went to the heart of the discussion, was to bring out the difference between Douglas and himself over the morality of slavery. He lost some debating "points," but he laid the basis for the voters there and then, elsewhere and thereafter, to make a rational choice between containing slavery and, ultimately, extinguishing it or extending it.

Exuberant supporters of Lincoln carried him from the platform after the Ottawa speech. Some Democratic newspapers reported that he was carried because he was made ill by Douglas's evident superiority.* The party press claimed victory for both debaters. Typical was the Chicago *Times* (Democratic) evaluation that Lincoln had been humiliated, and the New York *Tribune* (Republican) assertion that Douglas was "used up" by Lincoln. Douglas was not recorded as evaluating the result at Ottawa.

*Douglas attempted to make capital of the incident. At Freeport, he insisted that Lincoln "had" to be carried from the platform at Ottawa.

Lincoln wrote in a letter: "Douglas and I . . . crossed swords here yesterday, the fire flew some, and I am glad to know I am yet alive."

Probably Lincoln's managers felt a sense of relief after Ottawa. There had been some anxiety as to how he would fare in a head-to-head encounter with the famous Douglas, but Honest Abe hadn't done so badly. One farmer was heard to say of Lincoln: "I don't keer fur them great orators. I want to hear jist a plain common feller like the rest on [sic] us, that I kin foller an' know where he's drivin'. Abe Linkern fills the bill."

There was a six-day interval until the next meeting between the Little Giant and the Tall Sucker. In those six days the candidates went their separate ways. Even in their mode of travel there was the disparity that made their rivalry picturesque. Douglas traveled by special train provided by the Illinois Central Railroad, which owed much to him.* Part of the time he was accompanied by a vice-president of the railroad, a retired army officer named George B. McClellan, later to command the Union Army of the Potomac and to be fired by Lincoln for incompetence. Also accompanying Douglas was his beautiful young second wife, the former Adele Cutts, a leader of Washington society. Part of the special train was a flatcar carrying a cannon, which was fired to herald Douglas's arrival in the towns where he spoke.

While Senator Douglas and his party rode in style and comfort, Lincoln was practically hitchhiking from town to town. Sometimes he had to travel by circuitous

* It is not known how much of the expense of the special train was paid by Douglas and his campaign committee. It is generally agreed that the railway absorbed most of the expense.

routes in order to use the railway pass that he possessed as a railroad lawyer. One day the train he was on was shunted to a siding while Douglas's gaily bannered special sped by on the main line. Lincoln remarked to companions in the sidetracked caboose, "Boys, the gentlemen in that car evidently smelled no royalty in our carriage."

Soon it was August 27, 1858, and the speakers were at Freeport.

9. The Freeport Question

As at Ottawa, the scheduling of the debate at Freeport with plenty of advance notice resulted in such a crush that the town could not accommodate its visitors. The one sizable hotel, the Brewster House, was not large enough to handle more than a hundred guests. Of the estimated 13,000 to 15,000 attending the debate, at least 10,000 were from out of town. As at Ottawa, the visitors slept in wagons on the outskirts, on the ground near campfires, in carriages, and on the special cars on the railroad sidings. It was a big jollification. Lincoln had said he would answer Douglas's questions. Everyone had had time to read the questions in the newspapers.

It was an uncomfortable day, raw and damp, unusual for August. There were no convenient places for the crowds to eat and drink—no hot dog, hamburger or soft drink stands. People had to provide for themselves then. Some did so by roasting an ox in a ditch.

The holiday atmosphere was heightened by the banners and the marching bands, boosting the respective champions. Even the mode of travel from the Brewster House to the debate site near Goddard's Grove was an occasion for "creating an image," and was reported in the newspapers. Douglas's friends had arranged to convey him in a handsome carriage. Republicans, wishing to identify their man with the plain people, arranged for Lincoln to be driven in a Conestoga wagon pulled by six large farm horses. Unwilling to be remembered as a candidate in a carriage while Lincoln would be remembered as a man in a wagon, Douglas chose to walk.

As at Ottawa, where the roof had caved in, something happened at Freeport to make the crowd remember and talk about the physical trappings of the event. At this second debate, the roof of the platform leaked on Lincoln no matter where he moved about. The crowd would remember, too, that an old Indian chief shinnied onto the platform and seated himself among the dignitaries, wisely blanketing himself against the dampness and chill. And of course everyone would remember the delay while the shorthand reporter, Robert Hitt, was located and delivered to the press table bodily hand over hand above the crowd.

When he got under way at last, Lincoln promptly responded to the seven questions Douglas had put to him. He showed himself to be a moderate on the question of slavery, not a radical abolitionist as Douglas had implied. He was unwilling to disturb slavery as it then existed in the South, except in the District of Columbia. He would eliminate slavery from that federal jurisdiction if the voters agreed and if compensation were provided for slave owners. His justification for distinguishing the District from the slave states was that the capital was governed

Abraham Lincoln as photographed on August 26, 1858, at
Macomb, Illinois, the day before the Freeport debate. *A T. P.
Pearson ambrotype, courtesy the Library of Congress.*

solely by the federal government. The answers confirmed that he was pledged to a belief in the right and duty of Congress to prohibit slavery in all the United States territories, regardless of the Dred Scott decision.

There was nothing new in Lincoln's views as expressed at Freeport. He had stated the gist of them in earlier speeches. The predominantly Republican crowd already knew his stand on these questions. Now it was Lincoln's turn to put some questions to Douglas. He had devised them during the preceding week and had tested them on his advisers that very morning. They almost unanimously had urged against putting the second of the questions to Douglas. As in the "house divided" speech, Lincoln declined to follow the negative advice.

The questions were:

1. If the people of Kansas shall, by means entirely unobjectionable in all other respects, adopt a state constitution and ask admission into the Union under it, before they have the requisite number of inhabitants according to the English bill *—some 93,000—will you vote to admit them?

2. Can the people of a United States territory, in any way, against the wish of any citizen of the United States, exclude slavery from its limits prior to the formation of a state constitution?

* The English bill provided a choice for Kansas: if it adopted the Lecompton Constitution as written, it would be admitted to the Union (with a land grant commonly given new states) prior to having the population then usual as qualifying for statehood; but if it rejected the Lecompton Constitution, admission would be delayed until it had a population of some 93,000 (its 1858 population was less than 40,000). Douglas had voted against the English bill. Kansas voted down the Lecompton Constitution more than six to one, choosing free soil. It became a state in 1861.

3. If the Supreme Court of the United States shall decide that states cannot exclude slavery from their limits, are you in favor of acquiescing in, and adopting and following such decision as a rule of political action?
4. Are you in favor of acquiring additional territory, in disregard of how such acquisition may affect the nation on the slavery question?

Douglas's position on three of the questions was of relatively little significance. It was the second question and Douglas's response that together constituted a pivot upon which history turned. Douglas *might* have won the 1860 election as president if the question had not been asked and answered as it was answered, with the whole nation listening. As it was, the Little Giant had no chance to win the 1860 election after the Southern ultraproslavery political leaders read and reacted to his answer. Lincoln *might* have won the presidency in 1860 if he had not asked the question—but the fact that he asked it, and that Douglas answered as he did, placed Lincoln in the very center of the country's primary interest: what to do about slavery. It gave him parity as his party's spokesman with the Republicans' senior, better-known leaders, Salmon P. Chase of Ohio and William H. Seward of New York. It made for him friends within the party without making enemies.

In short, the crux of the national effect of the Lincoln-Douglas debates was the Freeport Question. It made Lincoln the strongest dark horse in the 1860 nominating convention because the delegates were willing to turn to him once they were convinced that their respective first choices—Seward, Chase, Justice John

McLean of Ohio, Edward Bates of Missouri—could not win the nomination.

The Freeport Question obviously was no accident. Lincoln had thought for a long time about the situation it represented. He knew what Douglas's reply to it would be. He had heard Douglas expound his views in Illinois, but it was essential to Lincoln, the Republican politician, that the nation know unmistakably what Douglas believed. A month previously he had written to a friend * as follows:

> Yours of the 28th is received. The points you propose to press upon Douglas he will be very hard to get up to, but I think you labor under a mistake when you say no one cares how he answers. This implies that it is equal with him whether he is injured here or at the South. That is a mistake. He cares nothing for the South; he knows he is already dead there. He only leans Southward more to keep the Buchanan party from growing in Illinois. You shall have hard work to get him directly to the point whether a territorial Legislature has or has not the power to exclude slavery. But if you succeed in bringing him to it—though he will be compelled to say it possesses no such power—he will instantly take ground that slavery cannot actually exist in the Territories unless the people desire it, and so give it protection by territorial legislation. If this offends the South, he will let it offend them, as at all events he means to hold on to his chances in Illinois.

The reason that Lincoln's advisers wanted him to omit the Freeport Question was that Douglas's predictable reply, that popular sovereignty could—or would—expunge the effect in a territory of the Dred Scott decision, would

* Letter to Henry Asbury, July 31, 1858.

be a vote-getter for Douglas in Illinois. It would be reas-
suring to Free-Soil moderates as promising a realistic
barrier to slavery expansion. Lincoln has been reported as
refusing to delete the question, explaining that he wanted
"to spear it" at Douglas in spite of the supposed boost
it would give to his opponent's reelection campaign. "I
am killing larger game. The battle of 1860 is worth a
hundred of this," he is quoted as saying.*

This statement would not necessarily mean that
Lincoln expected to be the candidate of the Republicans
against Douglas in 1860. It could mean that *any* Republican candidate in 1860 could use the Freeport Doctrine
effectively against Douglas—in short, that the Republican
party could elect the president in 1860.

Douglas, never one to shirk responsibility, was explicit
and unequivocal in his reply to the Freeport Question:

> I answer emphatically, as Mr. Lincoln has heard me
> answer a hundred times from every stump in Illinois, that
> in my opinion the people of a Territory can, by lawful
> means, exclude slavery from their limits prior to the for-
> mation of a State Constitution. Mr. Lincoln knew that I
> had answered that question over and over again. He heard
> me argue the Nebraska Bill on that principle all over the
> State in 1854, 1855, and in 1856, and he has no excuse
> for pretending to be in doubt as to my position on that
> question. It matters not what way the Supreme Court may
> hereafter decide as to the abstract question whether slavery
> may or may not go into a Territory under the Constitu-
> tion, the people have the lawful means to introduce it or
> exclude it as they please, for the reason that slavery cannot
> exist a day or an hour anywhere, unless it is supported

---

* John L. Scripps, *Life of Abraham Lincoln,* (Chicago, 1860), p. 64.
(reissued by Indiana University Press, 1961).

by local police regulations. These police regulations can
only be established by the local legislature, and if the
people are opposed to slavery they will elect representatives to that body who will by unfriendly legislation effec-
tually prevent the introduction of it into their midst. If,
on the contrary, they are for it, their legislation will favor
its extension. Hence, no matter what the decision of the
Supreme Court may be on that abstract question, still the
right of the people to make a slave Territory or a free
Territory is perfect and complete under the Nebraska Bill.
I hope Mr. Lincoln deems my answer satisfactory on that
point.

With that response Douglas was on the record before
a *national, attentive* audience, fully exposed to its political
consequences. That is precisely what Lincoln wished.

The consequences, as they related to Douglas's future,
might be good or ill. If, as he said, Lincoln had heard him
answer the question a hundred times from every stump in
Illinois, no one had paid much attention *until the Freeport
debate*. That was the genius of Lincoln as politician. He
had forced Douglas to answer—to reiterate—this time at
center stage, with all the apparatus then available for
spreading the answer to wherever people would read. It
could be recited, examined, and praised or condemned
by the Little Giant's friends or enemies in or out of the
Democratic party, in or out of the North or South.*

Granted Lincoln's shrewdness as a politician, there
remains the question of what he meant in the letter to

* Not for another century was there another comparable political campaign debate before a national audience. That was the series of televised
debates in 1960 between John F. Kennedy, Democratic nominee for
president, and Richard M. Nixon, the Republican nominee. Kennedy,
who made the more charismatic appearance, won a narrow victory. A
switch of an average of one vote in the 169,000 precincts could have
changed the result.

A contemporary illustration of the scene at Galesburg, Illinois, on October 7, 1858, at the fifth debate between Stephen A. Douglas and Abraham Lincoln in the senatorial election campaign. The campus of Knox College was the site of the debate. *Courtesy the Library of Congress.*

Asbury when he said of Douglas: "He cares nothing for the South; he knows he is already dead there." Lincoln knew that Douglas would continue to express the view that he firmly held: that local unfriendly legislation could keep slavery out of a territory despite the Dred Scott decision. It was a view that would win votes in Illinois, enough votes, Douglas hoped, to ensure reelection. However, at that point he was not certainly "already dead" in the South. He at the time was *persona non grata* with the president and with most of the more potent Southern Democratic leaders, but he had plenty of good will and considerable support in the South. As of the time of the debates, he continued to be the Democrats' most influential senator. He was the leader who had brought about the repeal of the Missouri Compromise to open the way for the expansion of slavery in the West. In fact, virulent antagonism to his Freeport Doctrine was slow in boiling to the political surface in the South.* Some Southern politicians, notably Senator Jefferson Davis of Mississippi, had reasoned similarly in public speeches.

The basic reason why Douglas was plagued by what he said at Freeport in 1858 was because already he was the front-runner for the Democratic nomination for president in 1860. Hence anything and everything he said in the debates were subjected to the most intense scrutiny, without regard to how many times he may have said the same thing in less conspicuous circumstances. Lincoln surmised that Douglas was "dead" in the South, but Douglas did not. For the next two years he courted the

---

* In 1860 Senator Judah Benjamin of Louisiana expressed the ultimate proslavery-extensionist disillusionment with Douglas in a Senate speech (*Congressional Globe*, May 22, 1860, p. 2241).

South confidently, and with some success. Soon after the
1858 Illinois campaign he spoke in Tennessee and Louisiana. The nub of his position was expressed in words
calculated to appeal to all but the extremists: "I have
never thought proper to disguise the fact that, if the
people desire slavery, they are entitled to have it, and
I am content with the result. But I would not be instru-
mental in attempting to force a Constitution upon an
unwilling people." *

Southern moderates were content for the time being
with Douglas's position—especially since he was in favor
of acquiring Cuba, whose climate and soil were favorable
to the institution of slavery. Not so the Southern radicals,
or ultras, who moved at once to deprive the Little Giant
of his power base. They deposed him as chairman of
the territories committee, which he had headed for a
decade. The radicals also were familiar with Douglas's
position on slavery as expressed in his answer to a question
put to him by Lincoln in the Jonesboro debate, September
15, 1858: "Would you vote for or against legislation for
the protection of slave property in the territories, if slaveholders demanded such legislation?"

Douglas had responded that he would not expect
Congress to protect slave property in the territories if the
local laws did not protect it. His answer meant that he
would not vote for federal intervention in such cases.

Taken together, the Freeport Doctrine and the Jonesboro Answer put Douglas in a self-contradictory position.
On one hand, he supported the Dred Scott decision as
legally blessing slavery extension. On the other, he asserted

* G. F. Milton, *Eve of Conflict* (New York: Octagon Books, 1965),
p. 361.

the sterility of that decision in the crunch of unfriendly territorial legislation.

This inconsistency was not lost on the South—nor on Lincoln.

Douglas's straddle, as Lincoln interpreted it, contributed to the unbridgeable division of the Democratic party in 1860. How could the slave masters of the South rely on Douglas as president? He was no Buchanan, a puppet to be manipulated by a cabal of cotton state senators. Better for them that the slave states secede and form their own nation than to have "nonintervention" Douglas as the president of a sectionalized Union.

In fact, the question of congressional intervention to protect slavery was a major factor in the bolt of cotton state delegates from the two-phase Democratic nominating convention of 1860. Douglas was nominated by the "regulars" after some of the Southerners bolted at Charleston, and more of them quit at the reconvened convention at Baltimore. The bolting faction nominated John C. Breckinridge of Kentucky. Further fragmentation of Democratic strength was caused by the entry of the Constitutional Union party, whose nominee was John Bell of Tennessee.

In contrast, Lincoln's position throughout the 1858 campaign was calculated to hold together the Republican rank-and-file moderates and even to attract some abolitionists who had no realistic alternative. He made no enemies. When the convention met in Chicago to nominate a Republican for president, Lincoln was the choice on the third ballot of a party untroubled by schism.

10. The Far-reaching Results

THE LINCOLN-DOUGLAS DEBATES deserve study as a model of political forensics. In historical perspective the Freeport Question and Jonesboro Answer overshadow the series as a whole. The only comparable political discussion in U.S. history was the Webster-Hayne debate about nullification in 1830.

Lincoln and Douglas were conscious that they were playing to a double audience. One was the audience of homespun locals with whom the candidates had to identify to win votes in the imminent election. The other was the national audience, which was interested in the Illinois campaign as an indicator of the nation's immediate future direction. The national audience, therefore, was more attentive to the speeches' substance than interested in the speakers' showmanship.

Lincoln projected the local, unsung aspirant, challenging the powerful, celebrated citizen of the world. He pointed out that, starting from similar circumstances, Douglas had won far more recognition than he. He compared his ordinary citizen status deprecatingly with Douglas's powerful role—one that could attract supporters by the promise of office. He nurtured his Honest Abe reputation by assuring audiences that he intended to expound principles buttressed by facts and to refrain from personalities and unfounded charges. He spoke of Judge Douglas as "my friend."

Douglas also assured audiences that he regarded Lincoln as an honest, intelligent man. Such polite preliminaries over, each found occasion to say harsh things about the other. Douglas accused Lincoln of "conspiring" to deliver members of the dying Whig party to the new Republican party and charged him also with a corrupt bargain with Lyman Trumbull, whereby Lincoln helped Trumbull win election as Illinois' U.S. senator in 1856 in exchange for Trumbull's promised help to elect Lincoln in 1858 to Douglas's seat.

The most serious accusation made by Lincoln was that of a conspiracy to extend slavery, with Douglas a party to the plot. Neither debater offered any proof of his charge, and each denied the other's indictment.

One tactic by Douglas caused Lincoln to use considerable time in several debates to defend himself. This was the allegation that Lincoln favored Negro equality with the whites—civil, social, economic. His object was to arouse fears that Lincoln's beliefs, if put into effect, would result in the colonization of Illinois by free Negroes. It also was meant to associate Lincoln with the ultra-abolitionists, who were unpopular in Illinois. Douglas contrasted his position: he was against civil rights for Negroes, he preferred to keep Illinois free of them, and in the territories he cared not whether slavery was "voted down or voted up." He also accused Lincoln of changing his principles on slavery depending on the predominant sentiment of the audience he was addressing. Lincoln's principles, he asserted, were "almost white" in proslavery southern Illinois, "a decent mulatto" in moderate central Illinois, and "jet black" in antislavery northern Illinois.

At every opportunity Lincoln emphasized that he had no intention of interfering with slavery in the states where it existed and that he favored enforcement of the Fugitive Slave Act, which even Northern moderates considered outrageous.

Lincoln argued that the only way to ease the nation's tensions over slavery was to adopt the Republican policy: to prevent slavery's expansion within the United States and to enforce the existing (but loosely enforced) ban on the importation of African slaves. This, he said, would put slavery on the path of ultimate extinction, which he believed was essential to the country's future welfare. He believed that the Dred Scott decision and popular sovereignty meant slavery expansion, and that slavery expansion would mean reopening the slave trade from Africa, because blacks could be bought cheaper there than from the breeding farms of Virginia.

Lincoln also spent much debating time countering another Douglas charge, that as a congressman Lincoln had failed to support America's effort in the war with Mexico. Lincoln indeed had voted for a Whig resolution to censure President Polk for beginning the war illegally. Douglas went beyond that and said that Lincoln had given aid to his own country's enemy. Lincoln focused his reply on Douglas's assertion that he had failed to vote for supplies for the American soldiers. Lincoln had, in fact,

Abraham Lincoln as photographed in Chicago on October 4, 1859. A *Samuel M. Fassett photo, courtesy the Library of Congress.*

voted for every such supply measure. This charge by
Douglas of what amounted to disloyalty upset Lincoln so
that he nearly lost his temper at one point. In Charleston
one of the distinguished citizens on the platform was
O. B. Ficklin, a Democrat who had been in Congress
with Lincoln. Lincoln seized Ficklin by the neck, pulled
him to the front of the rostrum, and induced him to
affirm to the crowd that Lincoln had voted unfailingly
for military supplies needed in the Mexican war.

The crowds at all the debates, though often partisan,
usually were well mannered. Now and then there would
be heckling and cheering. Douglas was hit on the shoulder
by a piece of melon at Freeport. Sometimes the candidates
would use a remark from the crowd as a peg upon which
to hang a particular point. Basically, however, the candidates were too conscious of the seriousness of the issue
to spend much effort on humor, invective, or other
oratorical "business." They were talking about the future
of the nation. Each was aware that the breaking up of
the Union was a very real threat. Each was anxious to
preserve the Union, but differed on the method. Lincoln
believed that confining slavery to its existing limits was a
national necessity and that popular sovereignty was a
dangerous substitute for the Missouri Compromise.
Douglas believed that the pressure for disunion would
cease if the South were assured of at least an opportunity
to extend slavery through the operation of popular sovereignty.

There was, in the last analysis, little on which Douglas
and Lincoln differed—but that little was at the heart
of the nation's troubles.

Each man had made approximately 60 speeches during

the campaign. Each had spoken an average of once a
day (Sundays excepted) and had traveled thousands of
miles. By the close of the campaign, Douglas was exhausted.
His voice had become barely audible beyond the first
few rows of the crowds. Lincoln had lost 15 or 20 pounds,
but was in good health. His voice was as strong as ever,
capable of carrying distinctly to the far edge of an outdoor
audience.

When the debates concluded in Alton on October
15,* Lincoln knew that he would be beaten for the Senate.
In a day before political polling had become a profession,
Lincoln had enough political contacts to know how most
Illinois elections would result. He knew at the beginning
that with only half of the state senators to be elected
that year and with the districts gerrymandered favorably
for the Democrats, he had little chance of electing a
favorable legislature short of a miracle. No miracle oc-
curred. The election assured Douglas of a legislative
majority. He was reelected to the Senate despite last-
minute Buchananite efforts to pressure the legislature into
another choice.

The Republicans, in fact, won most of the state and
congressional places, and outpolled the regular Democrats
by 125,430 to 121,609. The Danite Democrats polled 5,071.
This meant that prospects for the Republicans in 1860
were good. Results of elections in other states also
proved that the party was growing and that it was on
the popular side—the side of conscience—on the slavery
issue.

Still, Lincoln was somewhat depressed by the result

---

* The Alton debate was the only one at which Mrs. Lincoln was present.
Mrs. Douglas was with her husband the entire campaign.

of the election, because he just *might* have won, and he did wish to be a senator. Losing to Douglas hurt, especially because he believed he had held his own with that famous man. He told Herndon he was like the boy who stubbed his toe: "It hurt too bad to laugh, and he was too big to cry."

After he had watched from the gallery as the legislature reelected Douglas on January 5, 1859, Lincoln went to his nearby law office, sat for a while in gloom, then stepped out into the darkness, and began walking toward home three blocks away, along a hog-backed, slippery path. A foot slipped, and he fell, but he managed to get his hands down in time to break the fall. "A slip and not a fall," he reassured himself.

The dejection of defeat soon passed. Another chance would come for the Republicans, and perhaps for him. He answered Henry Asbury's condoling letter:

> The cause of civil liberty must not be surrendered at the end of one or even one hundred debates. Douglas had the ingenuity to be supported in the late contest both as the best means to break down and to uphold the slave interest. No ingenuity can keep these antagonistic elements in harmony long. Another explosion will come soon.

Back to the law circuit went Lincoln. "I have been on expenses so long without earning anything that I am absolutely without money now for even household purposes," he wrote to the dunning party chairman.

There are no records showing the cost of the 1858 campaign. Estimates tend to agree that Lincoln spent about $1,000, to which must be added the loss of income. The same sources put Douglas's personal expenditures at approximately $50,000.

As Douglas had anticipated, Lincoln gained prominence through the debates and the senatorial campaign that they highlighted. He was bombarded with requests to make speeches in behalf of Republicans. One speech, at the Cooper Institute in New York City on February 27, 1860, placed him high in the ranks of Republican presidential possibilities. That speech gave him favorable attention in the East, supported as it was by appearances in New England on the same trip.

Publication of the debates in the newspapers, and later in book form, helped to identify Lincoln as the authentic spokesman of the Republican party. The book, published early in 1860 at the suggestion of the Republican party organization in Ohio, sold approximately 100,000 copies and was used as a reference source by speakers.

Douglas expounded his views on popular sovereignty in an article in *Harper's Weekly* in September of 1859. It did his immediate political career more harm than good because it confirmed his Southern foes' fears that they could not depend upon Douglas to protect their slave interests in the expanding West.

In the 1860 presidential election, Lincoln won 180 electoral votes; Breckinridge, 72; Bell, 39; and Douglas, only 12. The popular vote was 1,865,913 for Lincoln, 1,374,664 for Douglas, and 2,814,968 combined for Douglas, Breckinridge, and Bell. Thus Lincoln did not receive a majority of the votes cast. He was denied votes of slave state Republicans because that party was denied a place on the ballot in those states. Lincoln did not cause the Civil War, but his election—on the principles of non-extension of, and the moral issue of, slavery—precipitated secession and thus, indirectly, the war. If Douglas could have had the nomination of a united Democratic party, he might have beaten Lincoln—but the premise of a united Democratic party with Douglas the nominee was not possible after the great debates. The events leading from the Freeport platform in 1858 to the inaugural platform in Washington in 1861 were discernibly connected. The views that Lincoln expounded led directly to his nomination in 1860 and to the winning of 180 electoral votes in his behalf by the Republican party. The views asserted by Douglas cost him the support of the South and led to fragmentation of the Democratic party.

At Freeport, Lincoln and Douglas were personal rivals for a particular office, the senatorship; but as the war began they were in accord that saving the Union was of first importance.* Perhaps it was to show publicly, in a symbolic way, his support of the burdened Lincoln that Senator Douglas held the president's new tall silk hat as Lincoln gave his First Inaugural Address. Speaking of and to the Southern states, some of which already had seceded, Lincoln concluded in language that Douglas must have heard with approval:

> We are not enemies, but friends. We must not be enemies. Though passion may have strained, it must not break our bonds of affection. The mystic chords of memory, stretching from every battlefield and patriot grave to every living heart and hearthstone all over this broad land, will yet swell the chorus of the Union when again touched, as surely they will be, by the better angels of our nature.

* In a speech in Chicago on May 1, 1861, supporting Lincoln's mobilization call, Douglas said: "There can be no neutrals in this war; only patriots and traitors." It was his last public address. He died in Chicago on June 3, 1861.

Additional Reading

Angle, Paul M., ed. *Created Equal? The Complete Lincoln-Douglas Debates of 1858.* Chicago, University of Chicago Press, 1958.

Beveridge, Albert J. *Abraham Lincoln: 1809–1858.* 2 vols. Boston: Houghton Mifflin Company, 1928.

Capers, Gerald M. *Stephen A. Douglas, Defender of the Union.* Boston: Little, Brown and Company, 1959.

Heckman, Richard A. *Lincoln vs Douglas: The Great Debates Campaign.* Washington, D.C.: Public Affairs Press, 1967.

Herndon, William H., and Weik, Jesse W. *Abraham Lincoln, the True Story of a Great Life.* 2 vols. New York: D. Appleton, 1895.

Milton, George F. *Eve of Conflict: Stephen A. Douglas and the Needless War.* New York: Octagon Books, 1965.

Nicolay, John, and Hay, John: *Abraham Lincoln: A History.* New York: The Century Company, 1890.

Sandburg, Carl. *Abraham Lincoln: The Prairie Years.*

2 vols. New York: Harcourt, Brace and Company, 1926.

Stephenson, Nathaniel W. *Lincoln.* New York: Grosset & Dunlap, 1922.

Wells, Damon. *Stephen Douglas: The Last Years, 1857–1861.* Austin: University of Texas Press, 1971.

POEMS

Lindsay, Vachel. "Abraham Lincoln Walks at Midnight," *Collected Poems:* New York, The Macmillan Company, 1943.

Stedman, Edmund Clarence. "How Old John Brown Took Harper's Ferry," *Poetry of the Negro 1746–1949.* Garden City, New York: Doubleday and Company, 1949.

Index